Heal me, O LORD,
and I will be healed;
Save me and I will be saved,
For Thou art my praise.

Jeremiah 17:14

LORD, Heal My Hurts

Kay Arthur

PRECEPT MINISTRIES, P.O. Box 23000, Chattanooga, TN 37422

Contents

A Special Note From Kay

Beloved Friend,

I cannot tell you how excited I am about this study. I have been so burdened, for there are so many people who are hurting and who need to know where to run to find true healing. It seems that not only is our society full of wounded people, but so is the church. Whether people know the Lord or not, I believe there is only one sure and permanent cure for all of our hurts. And that cure is found in knowing our Great Physician and understanding how to apply His balm of Gilead to our wounds. That is what our study will be about for these next thirteen weeks.

As you read this, you may be thinking, "But I am not hurting!" That is wonderful, but the world and many in the church are; therefore, what you learn from this study will enable you to more effectively minister to others. So press on! A ministry lies ahead—one which will have eternal value.

These thirteen weeks of study will require some digging into the Word of God on our own. How I pray that you will do it! Of course you can learn by passing over the digging that I ask you to do but will digging make a significant difference? I believe that it will. There is much in store for you...and I'm excited!

As you study the subject, "Lord, Heal My Hurts" there is one thing I want you to understand: This is a study which builds precept upon precept. Healing is usually a process that comes through the consistent and faithful application of the Word of God to each situation of life. It will take time for me to share everything with you, so "Hangeth, thou, in there!"

I have prayed much and send this to you from a heart of love given to me from the Father above, Who loves you with an everlasting love.

Ephesians 3:20-21

Kay

P.S. This study would be valuable for home Bible studies or for Sunday School material. We have forty-minute teaching tapes by me available for rent or purchase on audio and video tape to accompany each week's study. Also, there are cassette tapes to help those who want to lead a discussion class. You may write or call our ministry for further information: Precept Ministries, P.O. Box 23000, Chattanooga, TN 37422, (615) 892-6814, 9am-5pm EST.

WEEK
1

Why Am I Hurting?

My sorrow is beyond healing,
My heart is faint within me!
For the brokenness of the daughter
of my people I am broken;
I mourn, dismay has taken hold of me.
Is there no balm in Gilead?
Is there no physician there?
Why then has not the health of the
daughter of my people been restored?
Jeremiah 8:18, 21-22

DAY ONE

My platinum wedding band rolled round and round in a circle on the rec room floor, making a mockery of what was taking place. Tom was groveling on the floor, looking for my diamond engagement ring in the shadows of the table lamps. As I stood in the corner of the room, watching it all like a curious spectator, there were no tears streaming down my face. My lips were taut. No crying. No more hysterical sobbing. I was beyond that. As far as I was concerned, it was over. The wedding band had finally stopped going in circles. It lay dormant, just like our marriage. Tom was still looking for the engagement ring I had thrown at him along with my wedding band. He was murmuring something about how expensive the ring was! That made me sick.

I thought, ''You care more about that stupid, expensive diamond ring than you do about me! Don't you know what has happened? I have taken off my wedding band! The one you had engraved with the words, 'Our Love Is Eternal.' Don't you realize—hasn't it occurred to you—Tom Goetz, that it has never been off my hand since the day of our wedding?''

I would stay downstairs. The quarrel had begun in our bedroom. I didn't want to go back. For the first time in our six years of marriage, Tom had slapped me. The provocation of my tongue was finally too much for him. When the warm, salty blood from my nose touched my lips, I told Tom that that was it. It was over—finished. He had followed me downstairs, pleading. Now Tom would climb the stairs again—only this time alone. To bed.

Whether Tom slept or not, I do not know. I only know that the next day we called our priest, and he came over. It was cut and dried. The priest thought we ought to separate. I would take our young sons, Tom and Mark, and move back to Arlington, Virginia, where I had friends. It was that simple—on the outside. Inside an unseen but very real wound began to fester, its poison seeping into my soul. If the wound had only been mine, it wouldn't have been nearly as bad. I didn't know that the boys were hurting...they never cried in front of me.

My friend, have you ever contemplated divorce?

Have you ever wanted to walk away from a relationship? To say, ''Forget it; it's not worth it''?

Have you ever hurt so badly that you thought the pain would never go away? That it would be easier to die?

Or have you ever been so horribly hurt that you wished, or even prayed, that the person who had hurt you would just die?

Are you hurting...emotionally, spiritually, psychologically? Or do you have a mate, a child, a relative, or a friend who hurts?

What's the answer, the solution? Or is there one? Are some condemned to hurt forever? Are there some who have wounds so great that they can never be healed?

Or is there healing for what hurts no matter how bad the hurt?

There is, Beloved, because, whether you may believe it or not, you are beloved of God, and He desires your wholeness, your healing. About 2,500 years ago, God had Jeremiah record His burden for His people who were hurting. Listen to the anguish of Jeremiah's heart, ''For the brokenness of the daughter of my people I am broken; I mourn, dismay has taken hold of me'' (Jeremiah 8:20).

Why the anguish? Was it because of the greatness of their wound? No, Beloved, it was because there was a cure for their hurts, and they were not aware of it…or they knew where to turn, but for some reason they wouldn't!

Listen to Jeremiah's cry of dismay:
"Is there no balm in Gilead?
Is there no physician there?
Why then has not the health
of the daughter of my people
been restored?"

A balm in Gilead…a physician there…and healing for every wound of your soul. This is what this devotional study is all about.

I cannot wait to see, and hopefully to hear, what God does in this study of healing what hurts. Study diligently, and you will be awed by what God will do as you believe His Word and live accordingly.

I know. I have been healed, and so have many, many others.

May I make a suggestion? Find the Book of Jeremiah in your Bible. If you don't know where it is, there is an index in the front of the Bible. Look under the Old Testament books until you see Jeremiah and the page number on which it begins. Now, why don't you read a chapter or two? As you do, ask God to give you understanding regarding His people whom He refers to as "Judah" and what they were experiencing and why. If you are new to the Bible, don't let reading it overwhelm you. You will find yourself learning more and more about the Bible as we progress through our quest for your healing.

DAY TWO

I never thought I would ever go through a divorce. There had always been only one thing I ever wanted in life, and that was to be happily married for ever and ever, just like my mom and dad. I wanted to be wildly in love just like in the movies. I wanted an all-American husband who loved his wife and children, and I wanted us all to live happily ever after. I would have been content to stay at home, to be the wife of a successful businessman. To raise my all-American boys, to eventually join a country club. To play golf and bridge. To dance away the weekends in the arms of my husband laughing and enjoying the company of our friends.

Now after six years of marriage, it was all gone. My dream had become a nightmare. And it hurt. I had failed. The one and only thing I had ever wanted—to be happily married to one man until death parted us at an old age—was over. It had come and gone, and I was only twenty-six years old!

Oh but it hurt! But not as badly as it was going to! I was so self-centered, so bent on my own happiness that I never really comprehended how badly it had hurt Tom. He didn't want a divorce. We just followed bad advice given by someone in a clerical collar. Once the separation happened, the divorce seemed the natural thing to do.

Tom hated living alone. He would call me and tell me that he was going to a psychiatrist. When I asked him why, he said it was because he couldn't forget the awful things I had said to him. From time to time, because his hurt was so great, he would tell me that he was going to commit suicide. In my smart reply, thinking

I would bluff him out of it, I would say, "Go ahead and do a good job so I get your money!" His hurt became a wound—a wound that would go deeper with every phone call, every letter. Deeper until it became a rope around his neck and he was dead. Hurt and never healed. Never able to hear my cry of, "I'm sorry! If only I had known...."

For me, it would be different, for one day I would cry out, "Heal me, O Lord, and I will be healed! Save me, O Lord, and I will be saved!" I would discover that there was a balm in Gilead that could heal the sin-sick soul! How I wish I could have shared what I learned with Tom!

But then—learning to live with his suicide, learning to cope with the memories of failing my two sons by divorcing their father and exposing them to my ensuing immorality—all of this would be healed by this same balm and by my Great Physician Whom I would come to know as Abba, Father.

I have a message for you, beloved reader. One of hope, of life, of peace. Not my message, not psychology's, but God's! Whatever your wound, your hurt— whether it was mostly a self-inflicted wound like mine was, or whether it was a wound inflicted by others, God's Word says that there is a balm in Gilead, that there is a Great Physician there. And because there is, you can cry out: "Heal me, O LORD, and I will be healed; save me and I will be saved, for Thou art my praise" (Jeremiah 8:22; 17:14).

I believe that there is no child of God who cannot be healed of the deepest, most horrendous wounds if they will but learn three things: how to apply the balm of Gilead, how to follow the Great Physician's instructions, and how to give His medicine time to work! And that is what your study will be all about. In the days to come, the term, "the balm of Gilead," will take on meaning and deep significance as you learn how this phrase was used in Old Testament days.

May I suggest, my friend, that today you shut yourself up with the Lord for a little while and ask Him to show you if there are any hurts in your life which have never been totally healed. As God shows them to you, write them down. Or if no specific hurts from the past come to your mind, then possibly you encounter hurts you have to deal with from time to time. Write these down, even if you have learned how to deal with them.

Or maybe you are fine—no hurts: past, present or future! Then what are your mate's hurts or your friends' hurts that they have shared with you? Write out their hurts at the end of today's study.

As you write, please don't worry about what anyone would think. This is your workbook, Beloved, and what we are going to see is how God can handle and heal the hurts which come into our lives by the very living of life!

Therefore, when you are instructed to write something out, you will find it very helpful to do exactly that. There is a reason for what I will ask you to do, and I believe it will really help.

When you finish your writing, look up Jeremiah 17:14, write it out below, and then memorize it. I have found that the easiest way to memorize is to read something aloud three times in succession morning, afternoon, and evening. Try it!

DAY THREE

"My sorrow is beyond healing, my heart is faint within me!" (Jeremiah 8:18). Did Jeremiah pen these words to describe only his anguish as he mourned over the awful ravages of sin in the lives of his people? No, as it says in Romans 15:4, "For whatever was written in earlier times was written for our instruction, that through perseverance and the encouragement of the Scriptures we might have hope."

O precious one, after having taken a look at the hurts in your life or in the life of your mate or a friend, do you feel a sorrow beyond healing? Do you feel that wholeness is an impossibility? That healing is a miracle that would never happen?

Are the words from Jeremiah 8:18 your words? Could you have written them yourself? Do you sometimes wonder how you can go on? If life will ever be more than mere existence and day by day survival? Or are there times when you wish you wouldn't survive? When death would be welcome if you didn't have to instigate it yourself—or if you could be sure that death would really be sweeter, more bearable than life?

I understand. For the most part, my wounds were of my own making, and yet whether I inflicted them on myself through my own selfish and willful disobedience to the precepts of God or whether another inflicted them upon me, my wounds hurt.

Although the cause of our pain may not be the same, I have held countless numbers of hurting, bruised, wounded people in my arms. I have wept with and prayed with people who were so emotionally and physically abused that, if I had not known the healing power of the Word of God, I would have said, "There is no hope!" I have read their letters, and their pain was so great that at times I thought my heart would break.

There is nothing new under the sun. Some wounds may be deeper, more extensive, but pain is pain, hurt is hurt—it all throbs.

The wounds others have shared with me have run the gamut of hurt—from thoughts of worthlessness and hopelessness to feeling dirty, used, and cast off. Some have been so abused sexually, physically, emotionally, that they are tormented by the memories of it all—plagued by anything that recalls the incidents to the screen of their thoughts. The horrors of the past, the inability to cope, the feelings of never being good enough overwhelm and incapacitate them. They live with "if onlys"—"if only I had never married him or her, if only I hadn't allowed myself, if only I had responded differently, if only...."

And I understand. Don't you? Haven't you, too, allowed your mind to rehash the past, wondering what could have been "if only"? It's hell, isn't it? Constant torment as you go over and over it in your mind. I know. I have been there—but I have also found God's healing.

Although sharing what happened with Tom reawakens pain and brings tears to my eyes, still I can go on. I can live as more than a conqueror, and so can you, my friend. God has a way of escape, and we are going to find it. And your hurts are going to be healed, and you are going to be whole!

Today, won't you go to the Lord in prayer and let Him know exactly how you feel at this point about His ability to heal you? I believe if you will put it down in black and white and verbalize it that this will help. Don't be embarrassed to do so; God already knows your thoughts. However, as you address God directly, it becomes open communication which then can be dealt with in a way God designed. That way is prayer.

DAY FOUR

In the days of Jeremiah, the people of the southern kingdom of Judah found themselves in a distressing state. They were broken by the ravages of sin. Much like in our day, sin had taken its devastating toll, touching every level of society from commoner to priest to prophet to king. Judah was a broken nation of wounded people because of their sin and because of the effects of their sin upon society.

Some went about proclaiming, "Peace, peace," but there was no peace. They looked for healing, but it eluded them. What was the problem? This is what we want to look at today, for, as we do, we will eventually see God's answer. The solution offered in the days of Jeremiah is the same solution God offers for every age.

Before you begin reading Jeremiah, let me give you the historical context of the book. The nation of Israel had been one kingdom with Jerusalem as its capital until after the death of Solomon, David's son. When Solomon's son, Rehoboam, came to power, the kingdom divided into the northern and southern kingdoms. Under Jeroboam, ten tribes formed the northern kingdom, eventually making Samaria their capital. This northern kingdom went under the name Israel. Since they no longer had access to the temple at Jerusalem, they made themselves two golden calves, built an altar, and set up their own system of worship. Their idolatry continued until finally God sent the Assyrians down to take them captive. This occurred about 722 B.C.

The southern kingdom of Judah was comprised of the two tribes of Judah and Benjamin. Although Judah saw God's judgment upon her sister, Israel, still Judah did not learn from Israel's mistakes. It was in the final days of Jeremiah that God allowed the Babylonians (Chaldeans) to come and take Judah captive. The Book of Jeremiah describes the awful brokenness of this nation, the call of God through Jeremiah for repentance, and the ultimate destruction of Judah because they would not listen and be healed. In 586 B.C., the Babylonians would conquer Judah.

Now then, in the light of that brief history, read the first two chapters of Jeremiah. Watch how God talks to Judah reminding her of the days when He became her God (which, of course, was when Israel became a kingdom and before the kingdom split).

After you read these two chapters, look up the following verses from Jeremiah. Next to each reference, summarize what you learn about the situation in Judah during Jeremiah's time. Then as you record your observations, see if there is any parallel to our day. You might want to write the parallel in a different color of ink so that you can easily recognize it.

1. Jeremiah 2:1-8

2. Jeremiah 2:13 (Note the comparisons or contrasts in this verse.)

3. Jeremiah 2:17-19

4. Jeremiah 2:20-25

DAY FIVE

Before we get to the solution to Judah's hurts, I want you to do a little bit more reading in Jeremiah. If ever there were a book which Christians, the Body of Jesus Christ, need to study at this time in history, it is the Book of Jeremiah. If you will read it from the perspective of how the situation in Judah parallels the state of affairs in your nation today, I think you will find yourself awed at the similarities. I also believe, Beloved, that it will make you determined that you won't respond in the same way that Judah did to the word of the Lord which God gave through Jeremiah.

Let's walk through Jeremiah 3-5 together, and every now and then I will have you turn to your Bible to make a few discoveries on your own. I would like to have you read through Jeremiah 3-5 before we go any further. Please do not let this overwhelm you. Believe me, I do not want you to become discouraged in any way and perhaps miss the healing that will be yours if you will only persevere through these thirteen weeks of study with me.

Our study will be a process. Therefore, let me say from the very beginning that you will not find instant relief in a "one-two-three steps and you're healed" type of teaching. That, I believe, won't bring a lasting and continuous healing. I'm convinced, Beloved, that if your healing is going to be more than superficial, if it is going to be total recovery, then there are some crucial, fundamental truths which must be the basis of your healing, no matter the type of hurt. So, as I tell my Precept students, "Hangeth, thou, in there!"

Now then, let's walk together through Jeremiah. We will take it one point at a time.

1. In Jeremiah 3, God shows how His wife, "faithless Israel," has played the harlot.

    a. Read Jeremiah 3:1-13.

    b. List what you learned about Israel's behavior in the following verses:

        1). 3:1

        2). 3:6,13 (The heathen practices of worship in those days were often involved in giving homage to trees which were cut in phallic [sexual] symbols.)

2. In Jeremiah 4:19-22, you can almost hear Jeremiah wail in anguish, for he sees so clearly that the judgment of war and captivity is approaching. Read these verses and then note what you observe about the people.

3. In Jeremiah 5:7, God asks a very valid question: "Why should I pardon you?" There are many reasons why He shouldn't. These are given in Chapter 5. Read the chapter and list those reasons. Next to each reason, list the verse in Chapter 5 where you saw God's reason. Then in the second column, list how this parallels with today.

REASONS FOR GOD'S JUDGMENT   **PARALLELS TO TODAY**

Even with all of the just reasons God had for dealing with Israel in judgment, still this was not His desire. Throughout the Book of Jeremiah, you hear God calling the people to listen and to return to Him. Then, He would hear their cry and heal the people and the land.

O Beloved, as you study Jeremiah, you may so relate to "faithless Israel" because you have not loved God as you ought, nor have you lived for Him as you ought to have lived. If not, acknowledge your sin...but, my friend, know that God is still standing there in mercy, waiting for you to cry in faith, "Heal me, O LORD, and I will be healed; save me and I will be saved."

Turn and run into those outstretched arms of Calvary's love, and He will heal you.

DAY SIX

Have you ever stopped to wonder how some individuals can get so messed up? How can fathers and mothers give birth to children and then misuse or abuse that which they helped bring into existence? How can they abuse them verbally? Reject them, be mean to them, abandon them?

How can fathers sexually assault their infant daughters? To most of us, it is hard to comprehend. We don't even want to think about it because it is so abhorrent; yet, it goes on far more than most people realize.

Why do parents lash out at their children and abuse them emotionally? Why do they bounce them around physically, taking out their anger and frustration on someone weaker, smaller than they are? What causes a father to become so emotionally sick that he would do something like this to any child, let alone his own daughter? Have you ever wondered, ever thought about it?

Why do people become drop-outs on life? Why do they renege on relationships? Why do they become drug addicts, alcoholics, prostitutes, homosexuals, lesbians? Why do people get messed up in occult practices?

Why do people ruin their lives and the lives of others? Is that what they wanted from the start; what they wanted to do with their lives from the earliest time of childhood when they started to dream of what they were going to be?

I realize that the answer goes back to the problem of inherent sin and that there is no one, except Jesus, who has not fallen victim to sin by very virtue of the fact that they have been born in Adam (Romans 5:12). However, taking this into consideration, is this what sinners consciously plan for their lives? Of course not. People long for some semblance of "heaven," not "hell," in their lives.

Well, if this is not what people long for, then why are there so many wounded, hurting people who have experienced a living hell? I believe, Beloved, that the answer can be traced back from one generation to another, or picked up in the life of a single individual, to the fact that somewhere along the line, someone didn't listen to God.

As you read through the Book of Jeremiah, you see a nation of broken, wounded people. And do you know why they are in the state they are in? Someone "did not listen." And when people do not listen to the Word of the Lord, it affects families, which in turn affect societies, which in turn affect nations, which in turn can affect the world.

One of the key phrases in the Book of Jeremiah is: "Yet they did not listen to Me." The source of all of our problems as individuals or as a nation can be traced back to failure to listen to God in such a way as to believe and obey Him. Now that may seem ridiculously simplistic to you, but, if you will carefully read the Word of God in the context of the whole, you will see that this is the reason for our problems. Not listening to God is the way sin originally entered into the world. Adam and Eve did not listen to God. They listened, instead, to Satan and believed a lie. And what they did affected all future generations.

When I think of my first marriage, our divorce, and Tom's suicide, I know that I went through all of that because I did not listen to God. I did not do what God told me to do as a wife and a mother. I did it my way! But, you may say to me, "Well, Tom wasn't perfect either! If he had met your needs, then…" And I would go back and say, "But Tom had hurts from his family…." Then we would trace it all back to the fact that Tom's parents didn't listen to God, and Tom, in his trials, didn't listen to God. None of us did—and we all had the opportunity to!

Stop for a few minutes, Beloved, and think about your own wounds, the hurts which you have suffered. Why did they happen? Think about it and write it out.

As I have been writing "Lord, Heal My Hurts," I have been thinking about you. And suddenly it occurred to me that maybe you do not know much about the Word of God. Maybe the Bible has been a closed and boring book to you, like it used to be to me. Or maybe you've never even read it. Maybe you are like many who have come to our classes at Precept Ministries; you have come because you are hurting and are desperate for relief! That thrills me, and I am so glad the Lord has brought us together! You won't be disappointed if you are genuinely seeking God.

If you are new to the Bible and the words the Bible uses, then I believe I had better take a minute and define sin for you. Sin began in the Garden of Eden when the first man and woman disobeyed God. God told them not to eat of the fruit of the tree of the knowledge of good and evil. He also told them the consequences which would come if they disobeyed. However, instead of believing and obeying God, they listened to the serpent of old, the devil, and they disobeyed.

Sin, Beloved, is disobedience. To know to do the right thing and not do it is sin (James 4:17). Whatever is not of faith is sin (Romans 14:23). Therefore, sin is unbelief. Sin is lawlessness (I John 3:4). Sin's root is in turning to your own way. Isaiah 53:6 says, "All of us like sheep have gone astray, each of us has turned to his own way; but the LORD has caused the iniquity of us all to fall on Him." This, Beloved, is how the Bible defines sin.

Now then, let's continue walking through Jeremiah 6, 7, and 8, for we are on the brink of finding Jeremiah's solution to the hurts of his people. The solution will be mentioned at the end of our Scripture reading today, but it will not yet be explained. As we go through Jeremiah 6, 7, and 8, I want you to take the information you glean from the verses we look at and put it on the chart which follows. It will help you if you are doing this study with a discussion group.

1. If you have time, read all of Jeremiah 6. However, if you don't have time, read verses 6-19. Then note what you learn about God's people in verses 7, 10, 13, 14, and 19. Record your insights on the chart.

2. Read Jeremiah 7. When you finish, look up verses 8-10, 13, 18, 23-28, 30, 31 and record your observations on the following chart.

3. Beloved, when you read Jeremiah 7:1-7, did you notice the opportunity God gave them to repent? To repent means to have a change of mind. And a change of mind regarding the way they were living would bring a change in their lives, wouldn't it?

4. Finally, we come to Jeremiah 8. Once again, it would be to your advantage to read the entire chapter. When you finish, look up Jeremiah 8:5-7, 9-12, and record your insights on your chart.

5. Now then, what is the solution to their problems? Or to put it another way, why is Jeremiah dismayed? Read Jeremiah 8:21-22, and record your insights. As I said earlier, you may not understand the significance of Jeremiah's terminology in these verses, but you will later.

IN JEREMIAH'S DAY

THE PROBLEMS   **THE PEOPLE'S ATTITUDE**

WHAT THEY NEED FOR HEALING

DAY SEVEN

As so many have shared their hurts with me, how well I have understood Jeremiah's cry, "For the brokenness of the daughter of my people I am broken; I mourn, dismay has taken hold of me. Is there no balm in Gilead? Is there no physician there? Why then has not the health of the daughter of my people been restored?" (Jeremiah 8:21-22). Can you sense the anguish of Jeremiah's cry? It's apparent, isn't it, and yet, Beloved, don't you also sense that Jeremiah's anguish has come because he knows that there is a cure but the people are not listening?

There is a sure cure. There is a way to be healed, to be whole. I want you to know that. The people of Jeremiah's day did not have to live in despair and defeat, nor do you. You do not have to be crippled by the trauma of your past, to live as an amputee never again to know wholeness, any more than the children of Judah had to!

I honestly believe, Beloved, that there is no trauma of your past, no wound of your mind, emotions, heart, or soul that is beyond the healing power of God. Why? Jeremiah tells you that there is a balm in Gilead, that there is a Great Physician there.

Beginning next week, I want us to look at the Word of God so that you can see for yourself exactly Who the Physician is to Whom Jeremiah is referring. Then we will take a thorough look at the balm of Gilead. After that, Beloved, we will move on to specific hurts and see how these are to be handled so that there can be a genuine healing.

As Jeremiah looked at the brokenness of the people, dismay overwhelmed him because the people thought that they were doomed to a life of total despair. (Maybe you can relate!) The problem was that the people had forgotten they had a God Whose name was Jehovah-rapha, the God Who heals. This is why Jeremiah looked at their awful state and cried, "Is there no balm in Gilead? Is there no physician there?" To which the assumed, obvious answer was a resounding, "YES!" And from the way that Jeremiah then asked his next question, you know that Jeremiah's answer was the answer to their brokenness, their hurts, their wounds. Jeremiah asked, "Why then has not the health of the daughter of my people been restored?" (Jeremiah 8:22).

The ultimate source of your total healing, or anyone's, will be through the Great Physician and through the balm He has ordained. Therefore, won't you close this week by writing out a prayer to God regarding your healing, your mate's healing, or the healing of a friend. In your prayer, come to God in faith, and if your faith is weak tell God. If you think your healing is beyond His love, care, ability, or power, tell Him. Just communicate. You might want to incorporate Jeremiah 17:14 in your prayer.

WEEK
2

*Run To Your Great Physician,
Jehovah-rapha*

For I, the LORD, am your healer.
Exodus 15:26

DAY ONE

If your cry is, "Lord, heal my hurts," the Physician and the balm are all that you need. Healing is yours—if you want to be made whole. It may take time, but healing will come if you will only, in sincerity of faith, cry to your God, "Heal me, O LORD, and I will be healed; save me and I will be saved, for Thou art my praise." When you do, God will reveal Himself to you as Jehovah-rapha, and He will show you how to apply the balm of Gilead.

Let's look at the first occurrence of this name for God which shows Him as the One Who heals. Having just crossed the Red Sea with the children of Israel in their Exodus from Egypt by God's mighty hand of deliverance, Moses has sung his song of victory—"The horse and its rider He has hurled into the sea" (Exodus 15:1). Now the children of Israel have come to Marah where their thirst cannot be quenched because the waters of Marah are bitter.

Now that you have the context, let me give you Exodus 15:22-26, and then we will look at it in greater detail. "Then Moses led Israel from the Red Sea, and they went out into the wilderness of Shur; and they went three days in the wilderness and found no water. And when they came to Marah, they could not drink the waters of Marah, for they were bitter; therefore it was named Marah. So the people grumbled at Moses, saying, 'What shall we drink?' Then he cried out to the LORD, and the LORD showed him a tree; and he threw it into the waters, and the waters became sweet. There He made for them a statute and regulation, and there He tested them. And He said, 'If you will give earnest heed to the voice of the LORD your God, and do what is right in His sight, and give ear to His commandments, and keep all His statutes, I will put none of the diseases on you which I have put on the Egyptians; for I, the LORD, am your healer.' "

When God spoke to the children of Israel and said that He was the healer, He was saying, "I am Jehovah-rapha—the One Who is your healer." Have you ever seen God in this light, Beloved?

The children of Israel found themselves in a "bitter water" situation. like so many do today. The bitter water situation was a test. If you didn't see the word **tested**, go back and underline it or put a diagram around it. God wanted the children of Israel to learn an important principle: When things are difficult, you are to run to God. Listening and obeying Him would bring healing. God can take the bitter and make it sweet, because it is He Who is our healer. He was the source of their cure.

Compare their situation to yours today. When you have found yourself in bitter waters, what have you done? How did you handle them? To whom did you turn? Take a few minutes and list the various avenues you have taken or followed for healing. State whether or not they worked. Put down the why's and wherefore's.

DAY TWO

It is quite obvious from the Bible that the Physician to Whom Jeremiah was referring was God, for His name is Jehovah-rapha. *Jehovah* is our translation of the tetragrammaton, *YHWH*. *YHWH* is felt to be the most sacred of all God's names—so much so that the Jews used the name *Jehovah* as a substitute for *Yahweh (YHWH)* lest they blaspheme His name and be guilty of death. Jehovah is the name that reveals God as the self-existent One. How significant this is when it comes to understanding God as the One who can heal you. Since He is the self-existent Healer, your healing is not really dependent upon anything else but God! As you stop and think about that, you will find yourself breathing a sigh of relief, for there are no other factors that have to come together apart from God. He is the One Who heals (Deuteronomy 32:39).

Just recently I received a letter from a woman who is obviously hurting. She wrote, "Last Friday night you used an illustration in your message about a heavyset woman who ran down the aisle during one of your messages on forgiveness. She would not forgive her father for the sexual abuse he had put her through. Would you please share with me what you shared with her? I identify with this woman very much except that I never got pregnant, but the anger and unforgiveness are still there.

"It also extends into my relationship with other males, as I cannot form a friendship relationship with other males. I'm 37 and I can't get past this. But more important it causes serious problems with my relationship with the Lord. The word 'father' is not a good word. I hate it. When I try to pray I see myself standing in front of the Lord like I used to stand in front of my father. I realize the problem, but I don't know how to get past it. I love the Lord, but I don't trust Him. How do I get to trust and let those tall, thick walls down?"

This letter could have been written by anyone of thousands of women. How can they begin to be healed when the damage has been so great? How could they ever trust God when their image of a father has been so perverted and twisted by their own father? Some would tell you that they never could be completely whole. Others would say it would take years of professional, psychological counseling. But is this true? No, Beloved. It is not true, because God's name is Jehovah-rapha—the God Who heals. The same God Who is in the process of healing the woman abused by her father is the same God Who can heal you.

Think about it, Beloved.

DAY THREE

Rapha means "to mend, to cure." It is translated "to heal, repair, repair thoroughly, make whole." It is also used of physicians. Let me take you to one place in Genesis 50:2 where it refers to physicians: "And Joseph commanded his servants the physicians to embalm his father. So the physicians embalmed Israel."

Sometimes when we think of healing, we think of it only in the realm of physical healing. But does God involve Himself in healing only physical diseases? I could tell you, "No," but then you would be taking my word for it. As much as I want to be right, I could be wrong. This is true for any Bible teacher. This is why, Beloved, in our study I want to involve you in searching out God's Word for yourself. The symbol for the ministry I represent, Precept Ministries, is a plumb line. We chose this as our visual logo because a plumb line is an instrument by which you discern what is straight. The Word of God is our plumb line. If what we think or believe does not agree with the Word of God, then we know we are off the track of truth. For God's Word is truth (John 17:17).

Now then, with all of that said, look up the following references and note what or whom the Lord heals. In some instances, you may need to check the context of the verse. The context is the surrounding verses.

1. Deuteronomy 32:39

2. Isaiah 19:22

3. Isaiah 57:17-18

4. Psalm 147:3

5. Isaiah 30:26

6. Isaiah 53:5 with I Peter 2:24-25

7. Genesis 20:17

8. Acts 10:38

In the light of what you have observed from the Word of God thus far, do you think there is anything out of the realm of God's healing power? If so, be honest and record it. Then in the days to come, we'll see how God answers.

DAY FOUR

Let's reason together for a few minutes regarding what you have learned about the Great Physician. If God's name is Jehovah- rapha, the God Who heals, then that is what God does. He heals, and He can heal you. God's name is as good as God's person, and His name stands, because He never changes. God is the same yesterday, today, and forever. He has always been, and He always will be, Jehovah-rapha.

O Beloved, to whom have you run for healing? Make sure that you get godly counsel, that which has its very foundation in the Word of God, that which points you to God and all that He is, rather than counsel which is apart from Him and His precepts of life. Do not think that the spiritual part of you belongs to God and, thus, can be healed by God, but that the psychological part of you must be dealt with by man. The One Who created you, Who formed you—body, soul, and spirit—is not only your Creator, but He is also your Sustainer.

1. Look up and write out Jeremiah 17:5-6.

2. Now write out Jeremiah 17:7-8.

3. Now to solidify this contrast between the blessed and the cursed, either draw a picture showing the differences between them, or list the differences between them.

THE CURSED   **THE BLESSED**

We have talked with so many people who have gone to psychologists and psychiatrists, who in the process have spent hours of their time and hundreds or thousands of dollars, and who still are living as a dried-up bush in the desert, in stoney wastes, so to speak. Their psychologists and psychiatrists never led them to the Word of God to find the solution. They received counsel from man, but it didn't help, because man could only deal with the problem from man's perspective.

Then we have had the opportunity to take them to the Word of God, to teach them about the character and ways of God, to bring them to see the necessity of total surrender to Jesus Christ as Lord. And in the process of bathing them in the truths of God's Word, we have seen them healed. *Hallelujah* means "praise be to Jehovah or Jah"...and we say, "Hallelujah!"

DAY FIVE

When you examine Jeremiah 8 carefully, you see that Jeremiah was dismayed not only over the brokenness of God's people, but also because there was a balm in Gilead, there was a Physician there, but his people had failed to take advantage of either. Their wound was curable, but they were not accepting God's cure. In their trials and testings, they ran to everyone but God, and, therefore, their wounds were healed superficially.

They listened to every prophet that came down the road proclaiming his dreams and visions, but they would not listen to God nor pay attention to His commandments. If you would read through the Book of Jeremiah over and over, your eyes would come upon the words, "But you did not listen." They missed the balm of Gilead, because they did not listen to their Physician.

Because in Gilead there was a salve produced known for its healing and cosmetic properties, "the balm of Gilead became a proverbial phrase synonymous with healing. Thus, the Lord spoke through Jeremiah saying, "Go up to Gilead and obtain balm, O virgin daughter of Egypt! In vain have you multiplied remedies; there is no healing for you" (Jeremiah 46:11). The people of Judah had acted just like the world. In vain they tried to find healing for themselves, and there was no healing apart from God.

What a parallel there is here! So many have run to "Egypt"—a picture of the world and all that it has to offer—to obtain healing for their wounded souls, when they should have run to God as their Jehovah-rapha. They should have sought out God's diagnosis and cure for their hurts; they should have gone up to Gilead for healing. But they didn't! It was easier to listen to man whom they could see than to listen to a God Whom they could not see, Who seemed so far removed from man and his needs!

Thus were the days of Jeremiah! The Word of God had become a reproach to the people of God, and they would not listen to nor obey the voice of the LORD (Jeremiah 29:19; 42:13; 43:4; 44:16-17). And because of this, the whole nation, for the most part, was messed up. They were sick from the top of their heads to the tip of their toes. And could they be healed? NO! There was no healing for them, because from the prophet even to the priest everyone practiced deceit. They attempted to heal the brokenness of the daughter of God's people superficially by saying, "All is well, all is well," but there was no healing, and there was no peace (Jeremiah 8:10-11).

The prophets prophesied falsely, the priests ruled on their own authority, and God's people loved it (Jeremiah 5:31)! And the end of it all was awful. The people were never healed.

To describe their almost hopeless condition, God once again turns to metaphors by telling His people that they had forsaken the living water of the Word of God for the filthy waters of the Nile! Instead of going to Gilead where they could find refuge and God's means of healing, they went to Assyria and drank the waters of the Euphrates (Jeremiah 2:14-19)!

And what they did in Jeremiah's day, we have done in ours! We have drunk the waters of psychology, philosophy, and psychiatry instead of drinking the Water of Life! We have run to men and women trained in the world's universities, having certificates and degrees in counseling, but we have not run in prayer to the Child that was born, the Son that was given, Whose name is "Wonderful Counselor, Mighty God, Eternal Father, Prince of Peace" (Isaiah 9:6).

O Beloved, stop and think about it. Where do you turn first in the time of hurt, of need, of doubt? Write it out.

Now then, if you wrote, "To God," let me ask, "What do you do when you turn to Him? Do you wait on Him to see what He will put upon your heart? Do you seek Him through the counsel of His Word?"

God ministers through His Word. Therefore, as you learn to read His Word daily, you will find God speaking to you in incredible ways, miraculously supplying just what you need for that specific time—or bringing to your remembrance what you have already read.

If, however, you wrote that you turn to alcohol, to pills, to drugs, to promiscuity, let me say that these will not help you. They will simply escort you into oblivion as they lead you into sin's bondage...into bitter slavery and destruction. You don't want that, do you, Beloved? Of course, not! Then run to your Jehovah-rapha.

DAY SIX

As we talk about running to the arm of flesh in our distress, in our times of need, I cannot help but think about King Asa of Judah. Read II Chronicles 14. When you finish reading, answer the following questions:

1. What was Asa's relationship like with the Lord?

2. When the Ethiopians came against Asa, what did Asa do?

3. What did God do?

Now quickly (I don't want to wear you out! Hangeth, thou, in there; it will be worth it!) read II Chronicles 15.

1. What was God's warning to Asa?

2. How did Asa respond?

Finally, read II Chronicles 16.

1. When Asa finds himself confronted by the King of Israel, what does he do?

2. How does God feel about this? How do you know?

3. What kind of a man or woman is God searching for? And what will be the benefits of being such a man or woman?

Like King Asa of Judah, many in their hurts have not sought the Lord but the physicians (II Chronicles 16:12) and they are not being healed—or they are being healed superficially with Band-aids covering deep and putrid wounds that need debriding and healing with the balm of Gilead.

Who is to blame?

DAY SEVEN

Are you a victim of abuse? Have you been wounded, scarred, disfigured, and taken advantage of by man so that you are a distortion of what God intended for a man or woman? Was your childhood raped of its innocence?

Do you feel yourself caught in a web of sin woven out of the dark and frayed threads of rejection, anger, fear, and bitterness? Have you been told that you will never be free—that it's impossible to ever be the same?

Has anyone passed the verdict, saying that you will be confined forever in a prison of incompleteness because of what you have suffered?

Have you ever been told that you will be maimed for life—an emotional cripple or an amputee forever? That you will never ever be completely well, completely whole?

O Beloved, do not listen to the finite wisdom of man! Man is but man—limited by his humanity. His days are but threescore and ten! What does man know? What can man do but that it will always fall pitifully short of what God can do?

Don't listen to man! Listen to the God Who said, "Call to Me, and I will...tell you great and mighty things, which you do not know. Behold, I am the LORD, the God of all flesh; is anything too difficult for Me?" O ye men, ye women of little faith! "Turn to Me, and be saved, all the ends of the earth" (Jeremiah 33:3; 32:27; Isaiah 45:22).

As I say all of this, I cannot help but share with you a portion of a letter that I received from a precious woman who had been the victim of incest since infancy. She wrote:

"In a book I am reading, the author wrote of her personal experience with incest and how much her journey with God has helped her. The only thing I took discouragingly was her analogy of an amputee—saying that's how a victim is, missing something that can never be replaced. Several days ago I saw a Christian program on abused children and they expressed the same opinion. I must admit it hit hard at first. I felt my Light, Hope, and Faith pulling away from me for a moment, til I remembered what I read in God's Word about being born again, being a new creature, about all things being past and gone.

"What I got out of all this is that I'm slowly getting to be like Jesus. I have His mind. To me Jesus isn't a cripple, so I'm not. I am the only thing between God and being a whole person. I am the problem.

"You may correct me if I am wrong, but I'm holding out for all of God's promises. I will not settle to learn only how to adjust, cope, and function. I'm holding onto the promise of abundant life. I believe God can heal totally. I have the faith and hope that I will arrive at that point. That's my goal—to be all Jesus says I can be and wants me to be. Without that goal, if I believed what these two sources said, I'd stop growing. I'd settle, because there is no hope if I'll always be a cripple. I said you may correct me if I'm wrong, but you needn't do that in this case because I know I'm right."

Correct her!!! I wouldn't dare, for according to God's Word she is right! Aren't you proud of her in the Lord? Aren't you encouraged by her steadfast faith? I am...and I want to be proud of you also, my friend.

Take a few minutes to write out a prayer to your God. Pour out your heart to Him. Are you afraid to trust in Him, to call to Him? Are you afraid that He will fail you? Tell Him. It will help. Or if you want to trust Him, to learn to run to Him first, if you want your heart to be fully His, tell Him this. Put it in black and white. When you finish, read your prayer aloud to God. It doesn't have to be fancy or said in an eloquent way, only from your heart.

WEEK
3

There Is A Balm,
The Word Of God

He sent His word and healed them,
And delivered them from their destructions.
Psalm 107:20

DAY ONE

This week I want us to take a look at the metaphor, "the balm of Gilead," and see why it became symbolic of that which God would use to heal people. And as we do, I want to remind you again not to become impatient in our study. I know that sometimes the pain can become so great that you wonder how you can survive if something doesn't change immediately. O Beloved, it may not be apparent to you yet, but God is going to use all that you are learning week by week to effect your cure. Be patient. Give God time. All that you are learning will be essential for a permanent cure, so don't become weary and faint...or quit.

Now to Gilead. Gilead was a territory occupied by the tribes of Gad, Reuben, and the half-tribe of Manasseh. "Geographically, Gilead proper was the hilly, wooded country north of a line from Heshbon westward to the northern end of the Dead Sea, and extending northward towards the present-day river and Wadi Yarmuk but flattening out into plains from about 18 miles south of Yarmuk."[1] It was in this region of Gilead that a balm was produced which was known not only for its healing properties but also for its cosmetic benefits. To me, the combination of healing and cosmetic properties in one balm is interesting. Stop and think about it for a moment. Don't you know people who have experienced healing and who, as a result, have become more beautiful? Once the bitterness, resentment, anxiety, or pain is removed, there comes a new softness, a quiet serenity bringing new beauty. Think about it, and watch what God does through this study. Then tell me if you see a new beauty in those who are healed of their hurts.

Now then, because I want to keep taking you back to the Word of God, look up the following verses. Next to each, note what you learn from these verses that pertains to the balm or note where it comes from.

1. Genesis 37:25

2. Jeremiah 46:11

Gilead would apply to either the whole or a part of the Transjordanian lands occupied by the tribes I have just mentioned. However, Gilead was not only known for the balm it produced, but also within its boundaries there was a city of refuge.

3. Look up Joshua 20:1-9, and record what you learn about the purpose of a city of refuge. Write down the name of the city in Gilead that served as a city of refuge.

Gilead was a place where people fled in a time of trouble. Jacob fled there from Laban, his father-in-law (Genesis 31:21-55). The Israelites fled to Gilead when being pursued by the Philistines (I Samuel 13:7). And David fled there when being pursued by Absalom (II Samuel 17:22ff).

O Beloved, as a child of God, where do you run in the time of trouble? What is your city of refuge? Where is your Gilead?

Stop and think for a few minutes of how you have handled the traumas, the hurts, the wounds in your life. Make a list of the ways you have dealt with them and note whether or not you found healing. Be honest, objective. But do not despair if it seems as if there is no hope. Remember, there is a balm in Gilead; there is a Great Physician there.

DAY TWO

Yesterday I asked you where you ran in the time of trouble, in the hour of need. I asked you what or who your refuge has been in times past. These are important questions, Beloved, for so often we have a tendency to turn first to the "arm of flesh" instead of to our God. We can be quick to run to counselors, to psychologists, to psychiatrists, or to the reasoning, philosophy, or psychology of man, and, in the process, we can miss what God has for us.

Now as I say all of this, please do not add to my words. At this point, all I am asking is, "Where would God have you to run in the time of trouble or need?"

Remember when we examined Jeremiah 8? We saw that Jeremiah was dismayed not only over the brokenness of God's people, but he was also dismayed because, even though there was a balm in Gilead and there was a Physician there, His people had failed to take advantage of either. Their wounds were curable, but they were not accepting God's cure. In their trials and testings, they ran to everyone except God, and, therefore, their wounds were healed superficially. They listened to every prophet who came down the road proclaiming his dreams and visions, but they would not listen to God nor pay attention to His commandments. The words, "But you did not listen," are seen over and over throughout the Book of Jeremiah. They were not listening, and the balm of Gilead was the Word of God!

Now I say that the balm of Gilead was a metaphor for the Word of God, but how do I know that the balm of Gilead to which Jeremiah was referring is God's Word?

I remember the evening when I went to Him in prayer after reading this passage in Jeremiah 8. I felt that Jeremiah was referring to the Word of God, but I did not want to be guilty of stretching the Scriptures and making them say something they didn't say. Then the Lord led me to Psalm 107. I cannot tell you how excited I was! I was out in Dallas, Texas, and it was a Saturday night. A friend had settled me into one of her guest bedrooms, brought me a hot cup of tea, and left me to be alone with the Lord.

What luxury—a whole evening alone, uninterrupted, and in such beautiful surroundings! How I needed the quiet, the time to be with my Father, to hear His voice, to learn from Him. As I poured out my need to Him in prayer, He laid Jeremiah on my heart. When I came to Jeremiah 8, I knew He had heard. From there, using my concordance, God took me to Psalm 107, and I knew that I knew without a shadow of a doubt, without stretching the Scriptures, that I had a verse which paralleled God's use of the metaphor, "the balm of Gilead." And with that Scripture came answer after answer of how the balm of Gilead can be used to heal the brokenness of His people. On that day, in that guest room, God gave me the seedbed of the series I would later title "Healing What Hurts." The next day, I would share the basis for that message at First Baptist, where dear, white-haired Dr. Criswell had invited me to speak. How appropriate it seemed to me, for if there were ever an encourager of men, it was Dr. Criswell. Dr. Criswell, a lover and proclaimer of the Word of God, was the one who allowed our Precept Bible Studies to be taught in the church there.

Oh, what God has done since then as He has allowed me to teach these truths to others around the country! Truly, I have seen our Father heal wounds that man thought would never be healed. But then, isn't that just like the God of the impossible—the One Who said, "Call to Me, and I will answer you, and I will tell you great and mighty things, which you do not know" (Jeremiah 33:3)?!

Read through Psalm 107.

1. Color or mark in a distinctive way every recurrence of the repeated phrase, "Then they cried to the Lord in their trouble; He delivered them out of their distresses." (Each phrase need not be worded exactly the same, but must say in essence the same thing.)

2. There is another key, repeated phrase in this Psalm. In a distinctive way, mark it so that it will be set apart from the phrase you have already marked.

3. Now, list the various distresses God's people faced as related in this Psalm.

4. What verse in Psalm 107 would show you that healing would come from the Word of God and, therefore, would parallel the balm of Gilead? Write out that verse in the space provided.

DAY THREE

"Then they cried out to the LORD in their trouble; He delivered them out of their distresses" is a recurrent phrase used throughout Psalm 107. How very significant in the light of our subject—as over and over again the Psalmist describes for us the varied states of distress in which God's people found themselves. As you read the Psalmist's words, the tension builds—relieved only by the words, "Then they cried out to the LORD in their trouble; He saved them out of their distresses" (Psalm 107:13). Twice we read this phrase, and then we come to verse seventeen: "Fools, because of their rebellious way, and because of their iniquities, were afflicted. Their soul abhorred all kinds of food; and they drew near to the gates of death. Then they cried out to the LORD in their trouble; He saved them out of their distresses. HE SENT HIS WORD AND HEALED THEM, AND DELIVERED THEM FROM THEIR DESTRUCTIONS" (Psalm 107:17-20).

There it is! You have it! The balm of Gilead! It is the Word of God! It is the Word of God, the precepts of God that can heal the tortured, hurting, scarred, or embittered soul of man, woman, or child. You—or anyone—can be delivered from your destructions, your pits, because there is a balm in Gilead, and there is a Great Physician there!

How I pray you will wrap yourself tightly in the security blanket of this truth. I know that at first glance you may think what I am saying seems so simplistic, and you may be tempted to reject it or to think I am quite naive. I understand. However, give me a few minutes to think through why God gave us the Bible. I believe if you will hear me out, that God might use what I want to share in a really transforming way in your life as He has done in mine.

In John 6:63, Jesus made the statement that the words which He spoke "are spirit and are life." In other words, they were not like the words of man. God's Word is organic—life-giving—because it is literally the Word of God! God's Word didn't originate with man. "No prophecy of Scripture is a matter of one's own interpretation, for no prophecy was ever made by an act of human will" (II Peter 1:20-21). When you read the Word of God, you are not looking at man's analysis of God, Satan, man, creation, history, salvation, life, death, the future, etc. The Bible is not a book that originated with man. It is God's book, given to us through men who as they were "moved by the Holy Spirit spoke from God" (II Peter 1:21). In II Timothy 3:16 we read: "All Scripture is inspired by God." The Greek word for **inspired** is *theopneustos*, and this is the only time it is used in all of the New Testament. *Theopneustos* means "God-breathed." This is what makes the Word of God unique. Above all of the books in the world, it is the only book in all of the world that is a supernatural book, divine in its origin. That, Beloved, is why it is living—its words originated with God, and, therefore, God's words are exactly what Jesus said they were—spirit and life. The balm of Gilead is God's living Word! No wonder it can heal!

1. Read II Timothy 3:16-17, and then list the things for which the Word of God is profitable.

a.

b.

c.

d.

2. According to II Timothy 3:17, what is accomplished by the Word of God, or, to put it another way, what is the end of the Word of God, the goal to which it can bring a human being?

DAY FOUR

Since the Word of God is God-breathed, it is profitable for DOCTRINE. Doctrine is what a person believes, what they adhere to, the creed or truth by which they live.

If you or I want to know what is right and what is wrong, what is truth and what is a lie, then we need to see what the Word of God has to say about it—either in specific words or in principle or precept. Jesus prayed to the Father, asking that He would sanctify us in truth, and then He made this statement, "Thy Word is truth" (John 17:17). Anytime you ever come across something that is contrary or contradictory to the Word of God, you can know immediately that you do not have the truth. Whoever wrote it, said it, or taught it was wrong. That is all there is to it. To believe something that is contrary to the Word of God, or that in principle or precept contradicts the Bible, is to be deceived. If you embrace such a statement, you have chosen to believe man above God, and you have made the wrong choice. I do not care what it has done for you or for others. I do not care what supposed proof you have that the Word of God is wrong. I must tell you, you are simply deceived. Either God's Word is what God says it is, or it is all a lie. Because it claims to be God-breathed, it either must be God-breathed, or it is a lie. And a lie it is not. The Bible is the only book which, in its entirety, is composed of the very words of life, the very precepts of God. And if you are ever going to be healed, if you are ever going to be whole, then you must have the balm of Gilead, the Word of God.

Not only is God's Word truth—the doctrine or teaching by which we are to live—it is also profitable for REPROOF. The Bible reproves us, for it shows us where we are wrong, where we are off track.

God's Word is our plumb line by which we are to measure everything we hear, everything we believe, everything by which we live! Since I am not sure that you understand what a plumb line is, let me describe one. If you wanted to hang wallpaper or put up a wall and you wanted to make sure it was straight, you would drop a plumb line. A plumb line is a string with a plumb bob at the end of it that gives the line weight, thus, causing the line to fall in a straight line.

To check the straightness of something, the plumb line would be hung on the wall with the plumb bob on the end of the line. When the plumb line finally becomes still and stops swinging back and forth, then you would know exactly what is straight by following the line of the plumb line rather than following, for instance, the line of the door or window. Although the door or the window might look straight, if it didn't match the plumb line, you could know it was off.

Now then, how does this apply to healing our hurts? Some man or woman may come along and tell you that if you are hurting, then you ought to do "such and such." For instance, they might tell you that if you were hurt by your parents and are feeling suppressed anger because of their hurt, you need to get alone, pretend a pillow is your parent, and take out your frustrations on it. Or they might say that if you feel rejected, you need to go back to the womb, and beginning there relive everything you remember, etc. However, if the Word of God does not agree with the counsel you are receiving, either in specific teaching or in principle, then the counsel is not from God. Your counselors may be lovely people, well-liked, and well-thought-of. They may have impressive degrees and professional training in counseling. They may have helped others. But their counsel is not from God if it, in any way, is not in accord with God's Word.

As I say all of this, can you see why it is so absolutely vital that you know God's Word and that you allow it to dwell in you richly? Don't you see that what we really need is the Word of God so that it can keep us from ungodly counselors who would lead us into ungodly reasoning and unbiblical behavior?

O Beloved reader, let me close today with one question, and then tomorrow we will finish looking at II Timothy 3:16-17. What priority does the Bible have in your life? Have you given yourself to a diligent study of its precepts?

DAY FIVE

II Timothy 3:16 tells us that God's Word is not only profitable for doctrine and reproof, but it is also profitable for CORRECTION. And it is often in the area of correction that the healing process takes place. Correction is knowing how to take what is wrong and make it right. So often when people are greatly wounded by someone else, they harbor hurt and bitterness in their heart, nursing it rather than releasing it. They do not know that bitterness and unforgiveness will keep them from being healed. How often I have seen this! And, bless their hearts, when you point it out to them, they do not know how to let go of their bitterness. They wonder how they can ever forgive!

God's Word is so thorough that it not only gives us truth and shows us where we are wrong, but it also shows us how to take what is wrong and make it right.

And that, Beloved, is what you are going to learn to do in this book. And do you know what? If you will do what God says, it will work. You can be healed! You have God as your Great Physician, and you have the Word of God which heals. All you need is the faith that will obey and that will apply what you learn. And if you don't have that kind of faith, then you can pray, "God, I believe. Help, Thou, my unbelief," and He will.

According to II Timothy 3:16, the Word of God is also profitable for IN-STRUCTION IN RIGHTEOUSNESS. In other words, if you want to know how to live, if you want to do what is right, then the Word of God has the answers. To live righteously is simply to live according to the Word of God. And this, once again, is where healing begins—in doing what God says to do, no matter how you feel, no matter what you think. This, Beloved, is faith, "and without faith it is impossible to please Him, for he who comes to God must believe that He is, and that He is a rewarder of those who seek Him" (Hebrews 11:6). You cannot "out trust" God!

I will never forget a woman who came to me years ago, absolutely distraught because her husband was having an affair. It had so thrown her that she began seeing a psychiatrist. The psychiatrist told her that it would take two years of counseling before she would ever be healed. I remember sitting with her in the home where I taught a weekly Bible class. As we sat there perched on the end of the bed in a guest bedroom, I looked at that beautiful face, at her long dark brown hair, and her beautiful but sad eyes, and I wondered how any man could walk away from someone who was so lovely and so in love! After I had listened, praying all the time for the Lord's wisdom, I found myself reaching over and taking both of her hands in mine and saying, "Darling, you can be healed today if you will only believe and obey God."

Now, I wouldn't tell everyone they could be healed "today," for often healing is a process. But I would say to anyone, "You can be healed if you will only believe and obey God." We'll talk about that more in just a minute, but let me go back to my friend. She was healed that day, and that healing has lasted all of these years, even carrying her through more trials. When my friend told me she wanted to be healed, I opened my Bible and began sharing God's Word with her as it related to her situation. When I finished, we slipped from the edge of the bed, down onto the soft, blue carpet. The warm sun fell on our backs like a touch from the Father as we knelt at the foot of the bed and called out to our Jehovah-rapha. He heard. There we embraced one another, wiped our eyes, and got up from our knees. It was all right now; whatever happened, God was in control. My new friend was going to do what God said.

She went home, called her psychiatrist, and told him that she didn't need him anymore. And she didn't. I knew that for sure when she came to me several weeks later after our Wednesday Bible class and said, "Kay, I want you to pray for me. I don't love that woman like I should." What I saw in my friend was a desire to be like Jesus—and there is nothing healthier or more healing than that! She was willing to deal with this adulterous woman as Jesus did—in love.

Yes, Beloved, His name is Jehovah-rapha, the God Who heals. He is the Physician in Gilead, and you can cry, "Heal me, O LORD, and I will be healed; save me and I will be saved"—and He will heal, and He will save. I know—I have seen it in my own life, and I have seen it again and again in the lives of others. His Word is true. His name is a strong tower; the righteous run into it and are safe (Proverbs 18:10).

DAY SIX

There is one more truth we need to see in II Timothy 3:17. All that we have seen regarding the Word of God in II Timothy 3:16—that it is profitable for doctrine, reproof, correction and instruction in righteousness—has a purpose, and that purpose is that you and I, as men and women of God, "may be adequate, equipped for every good work." Vincent, a Greek scholar of renown, says that the idea of complete or adequate is "that of mutual, symmetrical adjustment of all that goes to make the man: harmonious combination of different qualities and powers."[2]

O Beloved, do you see what God is saying? He is saying that the Word of God can "adjust" us in all our parts! Let me go on, and then I will put it all together. The Greek word for **adequate** is *artios* which means "perfect or complete." This word and the Greek word for equipped is like a play on words. Equipped is *exartizo* and means "to equip fully, to accomplish, to thoroughly furnish." God is saying that the Word of God is really all that you and I need in order to be what we need to be.

The Word of God has the practical answers for all of life's needs! It will thoroughly furnish you for every good work of life! Vincent, in commenting on the words, "unto all good works" or "for every good work," says, "It is to be noted that the test of the divine inspiration of Scripture is here placed in its practical usefulness."[3]

Now, can you see how God can send His Word and heal you? It is because His Word is different than man's. God's Word is truth. It is alive. It can heal if you will accept it in faith and walk accordingly.

Oh no, Beloved, I am not being simplistic; I am not naive. If God is able to save man from himself and his sin, if God is able to save man from hell, and if God is able to make a person a new creature in Christ Jesus all through faith in His Word alone, then is He not able to heal anyone who will take Him at His Word? Of course! There is a balm in Gilead; it is the Word of God.

May God send His Word and heal you and deliver you out of all your destructions or, as destructions could also be translated in Psalm 107:20, out of all your "pits"! If life is the pits, the Word can get you out!
Memorize II Timothy 3:16-17.

DAY SEVEN

God is the One Who can cause all things to work together for good. He is the Great Redeemer Who will redeem all of your past and use it to conform you into the image of His Son. He is for you, not against you. And if He is for you, who can be against you? Neither death, nor life, nor angels, nor principalities, nor things present, nor things to come, nor powers, nor height, nor depth, nor any other created thing, shall be able to separate you from the love of God, which is in Christ Jesus our Lord (Romans 8:28-39, selected verses).

God's love is an unconditional, everlasting, transforming love. A love demonstrated and received at Calvary. And it is at Calvary that you, beloved of God, will find your Gilead—your city of refuge, your place of healing.

When Jeremiah asked if there were a balm in Gilead and a Physician there, he expected an answer in the affirmative! He had asked this question because he wanted his people to remember that God was the One, the only One, Who could satisfy all of their needs, heal all of their wounds, and provide them with everything they needed for life and godliness.

As you saw in your first week of study, in Jeremiah's day God's people had committed two evils. First they had forsaken God, the fountain of living waters. Secondly, they had hewn for themselves cisterns, broken cisterns, which could hold no water (Jeremiah 2:13). In other words, they had turned from God and His ways to the flesh and its ways. They did not draw from Him that which is essential for life—living water!

How typical this is of today—of our "Americanized" Christianity. We have needed healing, and, instead of running to our Father God and asking Him what to do, we have turned to man's psychology, to man's philosophy, to our humanistic version of Christianity, or to our own understanding. Like the Israelites of old, we have turned from the wellspring of all of God's sufficiency to the cistern of man's wisdom, man's ways.

A cistern is simply a place to store something—usually water. What you put into a cistern is what you get out of it! In contrast, a wellspring has an unseen source from which you draw. The people from Jeremiah's day had forsaken the fountain of living waters for cisterns, broken cisterns, which couldn't even hold water! And we do the same thing when we turn from the Word of God to the counsel and wisdom of man for healing our hurts!

O Beloved, I do not know how this book on healing hurts got into your hands, but I do know that God, in His sovereignty, put it there. He has a way to heal your hurts or the hurts of those whom you love.

Healed you can be if you will be healed His way! Healed you can be if you will run to Calvary, your city of refuge, which produces the balm you need, the salve that can cure your wounds. We will look at this next week.

Just remember that there is a balm in Gilead and there is a Physician there, and, because there is, you can cry, "Heal me, O Lord, and I will be healed!" We are going to learn how in the weeks to come.

WEEK
4

Calvary's Love...
Its Hell, Its Healing

But He was pierced through for our transgressions,
He was crushed for our iniquities;
The chastening for our well-being fell upon Him,
And by His scourging we are healed.
Isaiah 53:5

DAY ONE

From the moment she knew she had conceived, she had loved her son. She wanted to be a mother, the mother of a son. Now, as an adult, he had suddenly thrown up a wall between them. No more did he take her in his arms. No more did he come to her home. A wall was there, unseen but felt. A wall so high it couldn't be breached. A wall so impenetrable it could not be bulldozed down.

The pain was enormous. She could think of nothing else. He felt she had failed him as a mother. And she had. She didn't want to. It wasn't her intention, but was it as bad as he thought it was? Was it an incurable failure? One that would cripple him and their relationship forever?

The pain was excruciating. All of her life her goal had been to be a good mother and a good wife. If she had missed her goal as a mother, she had no other chance! The thought devastated her. She began to relive her past, analyzing what she could have done differently. Her despair increased. There was no redoing the past! She had wanted nothing more than to have her children and husband rise up and call her blessed—nothing more except to hear her Lord say, ''Well done, my good and faithful servant.''

My heart ached for her. I could understand the longing of her heart. I, too, loved my sons. I, too, wanted what she wanted.

Her pain was dull, heavy, always there, never ceasing. She told me that her pain reminded her of what she had heard about heart attacks—the pain was not sharp or knife-like, but crushing, like a boulder on your chest. Her heart had been raped, deprived of her son's love. The pain immobilized her until she ran in prayer to her Father God, her Jehovah-rapha.

It was then that God reminded her that He understood. He was a Father also Who had given birth to children. He understood her desire for intimacy with her child. Some of His children had cut Him off, had ceased to spend time with Him. They felt He had failed them.

''But, Father, You didn't fail,'' she almost yelled at Him, ''but I did.''

And then, in answer to her anguish, that still, small voice came into her mind, ''I know I did not fail, and I know that you were not perfect. But, remember, I am greater than your failures. I am God, and I have promised you—and your son, whether he believes it or not—that all things will work together for good. They will be used to conform him into the image of My Son. Now what are My promises that I have given you? Believe them. Live by them. You do what I have taught you to do. Regardless of how your son responds, you believe and obey Me. You cannot redeem the past. I can. Walk in faith. Either My Word is true or it is not—and you know it is truth.''

As my friend began to wrestle with whether her thoughts were simply a trick of her mind, letting her hear what she wanted to hear, or whether they were from the Holy Spirit, she told me with a chagrined look on her face that she finally gave in. The wrestling was over. Faith pinned her to the mat! She knew that what had been in her heart was in accord with the Word of God and the character of God.

How I rejoiced. My friend had run to the Great Physician, and He had given her the balm of Gilead. And although her situation did not change for a long, long time, she was no longer incapacitated by her sorrow. She found her refuge, her Gilead, and it is there that she dwells by faith.

This week, Beloved, I want us to look at what I will call the Christian's Gilead—a place of refuge where any child of God can cry out, "Heal me, O LORD, and I will be healed; save me and I will be saved, for Thou art my praise" (Jeremiah 17:14).

Where is the Christian's city of refuge? Where can we turn? Where is the place that we will find all that we need? Think about it today. We will talk about it tomorrow. If you have any insights, write them down.

DAY TWO

The Christian's city of refuge is the Cross of Calvary, for it is there that we can lay hold of all which God wrought for us through our Lord's death and resurrection. It is at the Cross that we meet Jesus as our Jehovah-rapha, the Lord Who heals, for Jesus is God, one with the Father. It is at the Cross that the veil is taken off of the Word of God, and we find the mind of Christ. And having the mind of Christ, we are able to lay hold of all of the promises of God which are yea and amen.

Your Gilead is Calvary's Cross, Beloved, and from it flows the balm of God's Word which is able to heal your hurts. It is there that you can cry, "Lord, heal my hurts," and He will, if you will take Him at His Word. There is no wound that Calvary cannot heal.

Now then, let me take you to the Scriptures and show you why I say that our "Gilead" is Calvary's Cross. Remember we saw that the word *rapha* means "to mend, to cure, to repair thoroughly, to make whole." The word *rapha* is used in Isaiah 53:5.

Look up Isaiah 53:5, and write it out in the space provided.

Isaiah 53 is a prophetic chapter which so clearly points to the person of Jesus Christ. Many Jews ignore a study of this chapter because they find it hard to explain away. It so clearly points to one person bearing the sins of others, and, as a result, justifying those people by bearing their iniquities.

The prophecy of Isaiah 53 really begins at Isaiah 52:13. Your assignment for today, which can be an incredible blessing if you will but do it, is to read from Isaiah 52:13 to Isaiah 53:12 aloud. As you read, each time you come to a personal pronoun such as "our" or "us," substitute your name.

When you finish reading the chapter, and substituting your name for the personal pronouns, write out the prayer that is on your heart in the light of this chapter.

ISAIAH 52:13-53:12

52:13 Behold, My servant will prosper, He will be high and lifted up, and greatly exalted.

14 Just as many were astonished at you, My people, so His appearance was marred more than any man, and His form more than the sons of men.

15 Thus He will sprinkle many nations, kings will shut their mouths on account of Him; for what had not been told them they will see, and what they had not heard they will understand.

53:1 Who has believed our message? And to whom has the arm of the LORD been revealed?

2 For He grew up before Him like a tender shoot, and like a root out of parched ground; He has no stately form or majesty that we should look upon Him, nor appearance that we should be attracted to Him.

3 He was despised and forsaken of men, a man of sorrows, and acquainted with grief; and like one from whom men hide their face, He was despised, and we did not esteem Him.

4 Surely our griefs He Himself bore, and our sorrows He carried; yet we ourselves esteemed Him stricken, smitten of God, and afflicted.

5 But He was pierced through for our transgressions, He was crushed for our iniquities; the chastening for our well-being fell upon Him, and by His scourging we are healed.

6 All of us like sheep have gone astray, each of us has turned to his own way; but the LORD has caused the iniquity of us all to fall on Him.

7 He was oppressed and He was afflicted, yet He did not open His mouth; like a lamb that is led to slaughter, and like a sheep that is silent before its shearers, so He did not open His mouth.

8 By oppression and judgment He was taken away; and as for His generation, who considered that He was cut off out of the land of the living, for the transgression of my people to whom the stroke was due?

9 His grave was assigned with wicked men, yet He was with a rich man in His death, because He had done no violence, nor was there any deceit in His mouth.

10 But the LORD was pleased to crush Him, putting Him to grief; if He would render Himself as a guilt offering, He will see His offspring, He will prolong His days, and the good pleasure of the LORD will prosper in His hand.

11 As a result of the anguish of His soul, He will see it and be satisfied; by His knowledge the Righteous One, My Servant, will justify the many, as He will bear their iniquities.

12 Therefore, I will allot Him a portion with the great, and He will divide the booty with the strong; because He poured out Himself to death, and was numbered with the transgressors; yet He Himself bore the sin of many, and interceded for the transgressors.

DAY THREE

Jesus as our Jehovah-rapha healed through His life, through His death, and through His present ministry of intercession. Before we move on in our study, I want you to see and understand how Jesus accomplishes our healing through these three means that I have just listed in the preceding sentence.

As we look at these, my friend, let me say that you may be wondering when we are going to get to the specifics of how to handle wounds that have come from various sorts of abuse—emotional, physical, sexual; from failures of the past; from words that have left what seem to be permanent scars; from rejection, etc. Well, do not despair. We will see how each of these can be healed. However, even the healing of these will work back to what we are learning now regarding the Cross of Calvary as our city of refuge. It is through Calvary that you have access to God's balm of Gilead as prescribed by our Great Physician, Jehovah-rapha. He alone is God, and He is the God Who heals all of our hurts.

Now then, with this said, let's go to Isaiah 53:4 where we see how Jesus healed through His life. In Isaiah 53:4 we read, ''Surely our griefs (pains) He Himself bore, and our sorrows (sickness) He carried.''

When you diligently study the Word of God, you will see that the best interpreter of Scripture is Scripture. When one verse explains another, then that is the interpretation to which we must adhere. In Matthew 8:17, we find an explanation of Isaiah 53:4.

MATTHEW 8:5-17

5 And when He had entered Capernaum, a centurion came to Him, entreating Him,

6 and saying, ''Lord, my servant is lying paralyzed at home, suffering great pain.''

7 And He said to him, ''I will come and heal him.''

8 But the centurion answered and said, ''Lord, I am not worthy for You to come under my roof, but just say the word, and my servant will be healed.

9 ''For I, too, am a man under authority, with soldiers under me; and I say to this one, 'Go!' and he goes, and to another, 'Come!' and he comes, and to my slave, 'Do this!' and he does it.''

10 Now when Jesus heard this, He marveled, and said to those who were following, "Truly I say to you, I have not found such great faith with anyone in Israel. 11 "And I say to you, that many shall come from east and west, and recline at the table with Abraham, and Isaac, and Jacob, in the kingdom of heaven; 12 but the sons of the kingdom shall be cast out into the outer darkness; in that place there shall be weeping and gnashing of teeth." 13 And Jesus said to the centurion, "Go your way; let it be done to you as you have believed." And the servant was healed that very hour. 14 And when Jesus had come to Peter's home, He saw his mother-in-law lying sick in bed with a fever. 15 And He touched her hand, and the fever left her; and she arose, and waited on Him. 16 And when evening had come, they brought to Him many who were demon-possessed; and He cast out the spirits with a word, and healed all who were ill 17 in order that what was spoken through Isaiah the prophet might be fulfilled, saying, "He Himself took our infirmities, and carried away our diseases."

As you can see, Matthew 8:5-17 tells of Jesus's time in Capernaum. Capernaum, where the Apostle Peter resided, was predominantly a Gentile city. As you read through this passage, answer the following questions:

1. What is Jesus doing in Capernaum? What is the focus of His ministry in this account?

2. Explain how Isaiah 53:4 relates to this passage.

3. According to what you have learned, when was Isaiah 53:4 fulfilled and how?

I will leave you here for today. Tomorrow we will look at Isaiah 53:5-6 and how Jesus healed through His death. There is so much to be learned, and it will prove so incredibly beneficial to your day to day living. I cannot wait to share it all with you, my friend—to have you see that there is no wound that cannot be cured through the Great Physician's use of the balm of His Word. There is hope, Beloved, so do not despair either for yourself or for your loved ones.

DAY FOUR

All wounds ultimately have their root in sin. Either we have inflicted and wounded others, or they us. Either way, it has been because of sin. Because we chose, or because they chose, to walk independently of God and His Word. Because we transgressed His Law, His will, His commandments. Because we did not choose to listen, to believe, and to obey God. Sin wounds. Sin mars. Sin disfigures. Sin destroys. And were it not for the Cross of Calvary, sin's wounding, marring, disfiguring destruction would be permanent, irreversible. But God! How I love those words, "But God."

In Isaiah 53:5, we read, "But He (Jesus, God the Son) was pierced through for our transgressions, He was crushed for our iniquities; the chastening for our well-being fell upon Him, and by His scourging we are healed." Healed!! Healed of what?

Once again, we must allow Scripture to interpret Scripture. Therefore, I want to take you to I Peter 2:24-25. Write out these verses, and as you do read them aloud. Reading aloud helps you memorize what you read.

Before we discuss these verses together, let me ask you one more question. What parallel, if any, do you see between Isaiah 53:6 and I Peter 2:25?

According to Isaiah 53:5-6 and I Peter 2:24-25, the scourging Jesus took at Calvary was God's means of healing you of your sin so that you could live a righteous life. Sin wounds; the Cross heals. The Cross heals, because it deals with sin. Therefore, Beloved, through the healing power of Calvary, you can live a life that is in accord with righteousness.

To live righteously is to live according to what God says is right. This means that no matter what has happened to you, you can live without bitterness or hatred. You can live a life free from that which would otherwise distort, disfigure, or destroy you. Bitterness can go; forgiveness can be received and given. You can be whole; you can be healed. We will begin to look next week at just how all of this is possible and can be achieved when we go into this aspect of our Lord's healing ministry through the Cross of Calvary.

Beloved, as you read the words, "Bitterness can go; forgiveness can be received and given," did something recoil inside you? Do you feel that you can never let go of bitterness? Do you feel that the wounds which have been inflicted upon you can never be forgiven? That you could never bring yourself to the point of forgiveness? That bitterness will be your lifelong companion? I understand your feelings. However, I would urge you to rest in what you are learning. Take it one day at a time. Keep praying, "Heal me, O LORD, and I will be healed; save me and I will be saved, for Thou art my praise."

If there is any bitterness or unforgiveness in your heart, write out whom it is against. And if you can, write out why. You need not be too specific if it is too hard to write out.

Finally, I want you to read Psalm 22. Not only did Jesus pay for your sin, but He became sin for you. What did all of this cost Him? Psalm 22 gives us a detailed description of what happens when a person is crucified. May I suggest that you read it prayerfully and thoughtfully. Also, if you are not really aware of all that Jesus endured for you at Calvary so that you could be saved and healed, then may I urge you to rent our video on this lesson. It has ministered so greatly to so many.

Now, considering all that you have seen in your study this week, list what you think Jesus experienced on the Cross when He was made sin for you.

DAY FIVE

If you are going to know genuine, lasting healing, then you must know where to find the cure. You must be certain where to run in the time of trouble. You must know for certain Who your Refuge is.

Remember, at the beginning of this week's study, I said that the Christian's Gilead is Calvary. Healing comes from Jehovah-rapha—from our God, our Savior, our Lord. When Jesus was on earth, He healed the sick and the demon-possessed through His life. When He went to Calvary, He healed us of our sins through His death. It is here that I want us to pause for one more day so that we might take another look at this from the perspective of Colossians 2:6-15. As we look at Colossians, please keep in mind what we studied yesterday.

Typed out for you is Colossians 2:6-15.

1. Read it through very carefully, and mark each reference to **you.** You might color it a special color or put a little stick figure like this 𝄂 over each occurrence of the word. When you finish, list everything you learn from this passage about "you" at the end of the text.

2. Now read through this passage on Colossians again, and mark each phrase, **in Him,** or **through Him,** or **with Him,** in another color or a diagram like this ∽∽∽∽∽∽ . When you finish, list all that occurred in, through, or with Him, as you listed all that you learned regarding "you."

COLOSSIANS 2:6-15

6 As you therefore have received Christ Jesus the Lord, so walk in Him,

7 having been firmly rooted and now being built up in Him and established in your faith, just as you were instructed, and overflowing with gratitude.

8 See to it that no one takes you captive through philosophy and empty deception, according to the tradition of men, according to the elementary principles of the world, rather than according to Christ.

9 For in Him all the fulness of Deity dwells in bodily form,

10 and in Him you have been made complete, and He is the head over all rule and authority;

11 and in Him you were also circumcised with a circumcision made without hands, in the removal of the body of the flesh by the circumcision of Christ;

12 having been buried with Him in baptism, in which you were also raised up with Him through faith in the working of God, who raised Him from the dead.

13 And when you were dead in your transgressions and the uncircumcision of your flesh, He made you alive together with Him, having forgiven us all our transgressions,

14 having canceled out the certificate of debt consisting of decrees against us and which was hostile to us; and He has taken it out of the way, having nailed it to the cross.

15 When He had disarmed the rulers and authorities, He made a public display of them, having triumphed over them through Him.

How does what you have observed in Colossians 2:6-15 relate to what we have been studying this week? How has this passage spoken to you?

DAY SIX

Have you ever stopped to think about what Jesus is doing right now? How powerfully the answer to this question was brought home to me when we inaugurated our Precept Bible Study Course on Hebrews. Before we ever release a Precept or In & Out Study to the public, we first work through it with our faithful students here in Chattanooga, or we use the study at one of our longer training programs.

When we began our study of Hebrews, I will never forget the insight Emily Farmer, our Executive Producer of our radio program, "How Can I Live," shared with me. A diligent student of God's Word, Emily started digging into Hebrews before I even got all the lessons prepared. She has been with us almost since the inception of our ministry, and so the inductive style of study is a habit with her.

When she gets excited about something, her lips purse up into an impish-like smile, and her brown eyes sparkle with joy. As I looked at her, I knew something good was coming.

"Kay, do you know what I saw as I studied Hebrews?" She didn't even pause for a reply, and I wouldn't have slowed her down for anything! "Jesus's work as far as our salvation is complete. When He hung on the Cross, He said, 'It is finished.' Therefore, according to Hebrews, His sole ministry on our behalf is simply to continually intercede for us! That is what He lives to do for us now! Isn't that wonderful?"

It was wonderful—awesome, really. The more I have thought about what Emily shared, the more it has ministered to me. I have gone to teach, and thought, "Right now, Jesus is interceding for me!" I have been witnessing and felt at a loss as to what to say next, and I have thought, "Jesus is making intercession for me." I have found myself in difficult situations, and breathed a sigh of relief because I remembered, "Jesus is interceding—that's all. That is what He lives for now." And I know the Father hears and answers His prayers. What a divine and incomprehensible mystery! What a marvelous reality to live moment by moment. Oh how I pray that I will ever be reminded of this truth. I am never alone in any situation—never left to my own wisdom, prowess, ability, endurance. Jesus is interceding, and, because of that, there is no situation out from under His knowledge, control, or purpose. It may be hard, difficult, but He is interceding and is able to save forever those who draw near to Him.

O Father, teach me to continually draw near. To snuggle in faith's security in your Sovereign will.

Look up, write out, and memorize Hebrews 7:24-25.

Are you hurting, Beloved? Remember "since then we have a great high priest who has passed through the heavens, Jesus the Son of God, let us hold fast our confession. For we do not have a high priest who cannot sympathize with our weaknesses, but one who has been tempted in all things as we are, yet without sin. Let us therefore draw near with confidence to the throne of grace, that we may receive mercy and may find grace to help in time of need" (Hebrews 4:14-16).

What a refuge we have in Jesus, our Lord Who heals!

DAY SEVEN

So often a person understands that salvation comes by faith alone in the finished work of our Lord Jesus Christ which He accomplished for us at Calvary; however, they forget that we are to continue to live by faith.

Somehow, we get it into our head that, although we are saved by faith, faith is not enough for our day by day living. Therefore, we slip back into a mentality of "I've got to do my part to please God" or "I can't simply trust the Bible. I need more than just the Word of God in order to live my life successfully." If we were to apply this type of thinking to the subject we are studying, "Lord, heal my hurts," we might think that we would need the insights, philosophies, or skills of psychology if we are ever to be healed. Others would tell some of you that what you have endured has scarred and maimed you for life, and, therefore, you will never be completely whole or healed. Or like the friend I mentioned several days ago, we might be told that it will take years of counseling before we can be healed.

To all of this, I must say, "What does the Word of God say? What does it teach? Is II Timothy 3:16-17 true; is the Bible sufficient so that the child of God might be perfect, thoroughly furnished unto every good work of life? Or to put it another way, does the Bible provide us with the answers or solutions so that the child of God can adequately handle anything that life brings into his or her existence?" From all that I understand from my years of study of God's Word, from my understanding of what God is saying in His Word, the answer is, "Yes."

My friend, at this point what is your concept of the Bible? Do you believe that it is as it claims, the very Word of God, God-breathed, inerrant in all that it speaks on, and the very bread by which the child of God is to live? Or do you believe that it is filled with myths, stories passed down around campfires from generation to generation, until they were finally recorded in a somewhat exaggerated way in a book said to be the Word of God? Do you believe the Bible merely contains God's words and that these can be sorted out and declared to be His words or not His words by theological scholars? Or do you believe the Bible to be only God's Word as it personally speaks or relates to you in a spiritual sense?

What do you believe about the Word of God? Write it out, and then look up the following verses to see what God says regarding His Word, the Bible.

Write out each verse or, if you prefer, the essence of what the verse says. I will leave out II Timothy 3:16-17 since we have covered it; however, don't forget what it says.

1. II Peter 1:20-21

2. Luke 24:25-27

3. Isaiah 8:20

4. John 17:17

5. John 6:63

I leave you with these verses, Beloved, and with the question, "Whose word are you going to accept regarding the Word of God, man's or God's?"

WEEK
5

*Are You Free
To Choose?*

*Even so consider yourselves to be dead to sin,
but alive to God in Christ Jesus.*
Romans 6:11

DAY ONE

One cannot speak of the crucifixion of our Lord Jesus Christ apart from His resurrection from the dead, for if there were no resurrection, then mankind—which includes you and me—would still be dead in our trespasses and sins. The bodily resurrection of our Lord is an essential ingredient of the gospel. If the dead are not raised, then we are without hope. It is the resurrection that gives us newness of life. This we are going to see very clearly in our forthcoming study of Romans 6, all of which is essential to your healing from sin's otherwise destructive inflictions.

However, Beloved, before we look at Romans 6, I want to make sure you understand the significance of the resurrection and exactly how one is saved.

The resurrection of our Lord Jesus Christ testifies to two vital truths. First, it shows that God was propitiated, or satisfied, with the substitutionary death of our Lord, as Jesus became the bearer of our sins. In Romans 4:25, we read: ''He who was delivered up because of our transgressions, and was raised because of our justification.'' ''Raised because of our justification'' means that, because of Jesus's adequate payment for our sins through the shedding of His own sinless blood, God could declare us righteous, justified in His sight. Jesus was raised from the dead because His death satisfied the righteousness of our holy God.

The second thing Jesus's resurrection shows us is that Jesus Christ conquered death. Death's hold over man was because of his sin. However, once sin is paid for, death no longer has any holding power. ''The sting of death is sin, and the power of sin is the law'' (I Corinthians 15:56). Jesus redeemed us from the curse of the Law in His death by becoming a curse for us, thereby taking care of the power of sin. Jesus also took the stinger out of death by paying for our sin. Therefore, because our sin is paid for in full, death has no power over us.

''Since then the children share in flesh and blood, He Himself likewise also partook of the same, that through death He might render powerless him who had the power of death, that is, the devil; and might deliver those who through fear of death were subject to slavery all their lives'' (Hebrews 2:14-15). Satan can never hold a child of God in death's chains because all of his sin is covered by the blood of Jesus Christ. Therefore, resurrection is inevitable. For a Christian, death is ''to be absent from the body and to be at home with the Lord'' (II Corinthians 5:8). ''To live is Christ, and to die is gain'' for the child of God (Philippians 1:21).

O Beloved, if you are a child of God, one thing of which you can be absolutely sure is that you never need to fear death. The moment you close your eyes on earth, you will behold, in person, the Lover of your soul, the Healer of all your wounds, the One Who says that you are precious in His sight.

I say all of this regarding salvation, and yet, Beloved, I cannot go any further until I am sure that you comprehend exactly where you stand with God. Is He truly your heavenly Father? Have you really believed on the Lord Jesus Christ? I ask this not to cause you to doubt a salvation that is real, but to cause you to examine yourself to see if you are in the faith, for apart from salvation I believe you will never really know a permanent healing of your wounds. Therefore, for you to cry out, ''Heal me, O Lord,'' without first having cried out to the Christ of Calvary, ''Save me, O Lord,'' would, in my estimation, be futile. Metaphorically speaking, the Cross becomes our Gilead from which flows our Lord's healing balm.

Salvation, the kingdom of heaven, belongs to the poor in spirit. Matthew 5:3 says, "Blessed are the poor in spirit, for theirs is the kingdom of heaven." To be poor in spirit is to recognize that you are spiritually destitute and, therefore, totally incapable of meriting or earning salvation in any way. To see that, in and of yourself, you cannot help yourself nor vindicate yourself in any way with respect to your sin is to be poor in spirit. In I Timothy, Paul wrote under the leadership of the Spirit of God the unwavering and blessed truth that Christ Jesus came into the world to save sinners (1:15). It is those who are poor in spirit who understand that they are sinners, totally impotent to please or serve God.

I think poverty of spirit is interwoven in the act of repentance. Repentance is a change of mind. With respect to salvation, it is a change of mind regarding self! To repent is to see yourself as you really are and to change your mind in respect to your relationship to God the Father and to His Son the Lord Jesus Christ. In repentance one sees sin as it is and wants to be free from it. Of course, freedom from sin only comes by believing on the Lord Jesus Christ, for the one who commits sin is the slave of sin (John 8:34). However, if the Son shall set you free, you shall be free indeed (John 8:36).

The poor in spirit see that freedom from sin is impossible in and of themselves and apart from the saving grace of our Lord Jesus Christ; they see freedom is possible only through His substitutionary death for us.

Think on these things, Beloved, and then tomorrow I want to share with you how I came to salvation.

DAY TWO

Before you came to understand your sin, repent, and believe on the Lord Jesus Christ, did you ever feel as if you couldn't be good even if you wanted to? Did you ever hate the things you were doing, try to stop, but couldn't? I understand. That is exactly the way it was for me. After I left Tom, I went into an immoral life style going from one man to another in search of someone who would love me unconditionally. I didn't know God's Word said that the committing of a sin would make me a slave to it. I wasn't saved until I was twenty-nine.

As I look back now, I so clearly see the awful chains that shackled me to sin. I remember when I finally faced my immorality for what it was. I saw that I could no longer excuse my behavior by society's acceptance of it. What others did was not always right. My mom and dad had taught me that as a young child. No, my immorality would not be deemed excusable because others were immoral.

In that mystery of grace not yet recognized, I finally saw that someday I would stand before a holy God and justly hear, "Depart from Me into everlasting fire." I hadn't been taught about the reality and certainty of hell for all of those who did not have the Son of God residing within by faith. I didn't even fear hell at that point. I simply knew that a holy God could not condone my immorality and, therefore, could not accept me into heaven.

Therefore, I determined I would quit being immoral. I decided I would change my life style. And try I did. But it didn't work. I would say, "I'm not going to do that anymore." But I would! I would go out and be immoral again. So once again,

I would resolve, "I'm not going to do it anymore," but I would. Little did I realize how well I would someday relate to Paul's cry, "Wretched man that I am! Who will set me free from the body of this death?" (Romans 7:24). I was a slave to sin. I was not poor in spirit; I thought I could set myself free. I didn't know that slaves couldn't do that. I made resolution after resolution, but resolutions could not unlock the chains that bound me. I felt sick. At the time, I was working as a registered nurse on a research team at Johns Hopkins, and I remember thinking, "I have a sickness no one can cure!" My sickness was of the soul, not the body. "Oh," I groaned, "if only I were physically sick!"

When I woke up the morning of July 16, 1963, I thought, "I cannot go to work. I'm too ill—ill with a sickness that cannot be cured." I called the doctor I worked for and told him that I would see him on Monday. I dragged into the kitchen to bake a cake. I thought, "I'll take the boys camping." Camping with the boys was a means to an end; I wanted them to know that I loved them, that I cared, that they were special to me. I craved being a perfect mother to them. But even here, I had failed. They didn't have a normal family life. Mothers shouldn't be dating; they should be living with Father! And I had left their father!

As I put the cake into the oven, Mark, hungry for his mommy's love, was clinging to my apron. Suddenly I bent down, looked into his precious little eyes, and, in words trembling with emotion, I stammered, "Mark, honey, Mommy has to be alone for a few minutes. Will you let me be alone just for a minute or two?"

I thought he could sense the urgency of my request as his little blond head bobbed up and down; yet, I had to be sure, so I asked once again, "Will you let Mommy be alone for just a few minutes?" And with that, I ran out of the kitchen.

My hand grabbed the banister in my living room, propelling me up the stairs to my bedroom. I took the stairs two at a time—I had to be alone. My bed was my destination. When I entered the room, I just missed the night stand as I collapsed on my knees. I had to get there in a hurry before my heart ruptured. I couldn't contain my cry any longer.

"O God, I don't care what You do to me," I sobbed as I spilled out the worst things I thought could ever happen to me. "I don't care if You paralyze me from the neck down. I don't care if I never see another man as long as I live. I don't care what You do to my two boys...if You will only give me peace."

That was all I prayed. There, on my knees, I received the Prince of Peace. I didn't know at the time that this was what God called salvation. I only knew that I was clean—and that Jesus was with me, and that wherever I went He would go with me.

In the days that followed, I knew I had been set free. My perspective on life was different. I had a hunger for the Word of God. And, wonder of wonders, I could understand it. It was as if someone had taken a veil off it! I was no longer a slave. I had the power to say "No!" to sin and to live according to God's commandments. It was as if a lawkeeper had taken up residence within me! And, of course, He had! His name was the Lord Jesus Christ. Oh, I'm not saying that I didn't sin. I did, but not like I used to! Now sin was a matter of free choice, and sin was not something I casually chose! I wanted to please my God. And that I was able to do, because the Godhead had taken up residence within (John 14:23).

I was healed of sin. I, who at one time had thought that God was lucky to have me on His team doing church work, had finally seen my total poverty of spirit. I was willing to deny myself, take up my cross, and follow Him. And when I finally did, I found my Gilead at the foot of the Cross.

O Beloved, have you come to the end of self? Have you seen your total impotence, your total unworthiness? Have you seen your nothingness apart from God? And have you seen Jesus, God the Son, Who left heaven to take upon Himself flesh and blood that He might taste death for you and for all mankind? Do you believe that? Do you believe that He died in your stead, that He was made sin for you, so that you, a hopeless, helpless, sinful enemy of God, might have His righteousness and His life? Have you repented—turned from self—to believe on the Lord Jesus Christ? Have you been saved from your sin? If you haven't, then genuine, lasting healing can never be yours until you do.

Why delay, beloved unbeliever? Come to Him. Call upon His name. Believe in your heart that God has raised Jesus from the dead. Confess the Lord Jesus Christ, and you will be saved, "for with the heart man believes, resulting in righteousness, and with the mouth he confesses, resulting in salvation. For the Scripture says, 'Whoever believes in Him will not be disappointed.' For there is no distinction between Jew and Greek (Gentile); for the same Lord is Lord of all, abounding in riches for all who call upon Him; for 'whoever will call upon the name of the Lord will be saved' " (Romans 10:10-13).

What is your response? Record it, Beloved.

DAY THREE

I have been talking, and you haven't had any written assignments. Today there is much to see regarding your freedom as a child of God from slavery to sin.

I want you to observe and meditate upon Romans 6. (To meditate is to think upon something, to seek to understand it. Notice, please, I am urging you to biblical meditation—not what the world calls you to do.) To me, Romans 6, 7, and 8 are three of the most significant chapters in all of the Word of God. Romans 6 is typed out for you. Read it through once rapidly without stopping to ponder its intricacies. Then read it again carefully and prayerfully as many times as possible. Read it aloud.

ROMANS CHAPTER SIX

1 What shall we say then? Are we to continue in sin that grace might increase?

2 May it never be! How shall we who died to sin still live in it?

3 Or do you not know that all of us who have been baptized into Christ Jesus have been baptized into His death?

4 Therefore we have been buried with Him through baptism into death, in order that as Christ was raised from the dead through the glory of the Father, so we too might walk in newness of life.

5 For if we have become united with Him in the likeness of His death, certainly we shall be also in the likeness of His resurrection,

6 knowing this, that our old self was crucified with Him, that our body of sin might be done away with, that we should no longer be slaves to sin;

7 for he who has died is freed from sin.

8 Now if we have died with Christ, we believe that we shall also live with Him,

9 knowing that Christ, having been raised from the dead, is never to die again; death no longer is master over Him.

10 For the death that He died, He died to sin, once for all; but the life that He lives, He lives to God.

11 Even so consider yourselves to be dead to sin, but alive to God in Christ Jesus.

12 Therefore do not let sin reign in your mortal body that you should obey its lusts,

13 and do not go on presenting the members of your body to sin as instruments of unrighteousness; but present yourselves to God as those alive from the dead, and your members as instruments of righteousness to God.

14 For sin shall not be master over you, for you are not under law, but under grace.

15 What then? Shall we sin because we are not under law but under grace? May it never be!

16 Do you not know that when you present yourselves to someone as slaves for obedience, you are slaves of the one whom you obey, either of sin resulting in death, or of obedience resulting in righteousness?

17 But thanks be to God that though you were slaves of sin, you became obedient from the heart to that form of teaching to which you were committed,

18 and having been freed from sin, you became slaves of righteousness.

19 I am speaking in human terms because of the weakness of your flesh. For just as you presented your members as slaves to impurity and to lawlessness, resulting in further lawlessness, so now present your members as slaves to righteousness, resulting in sanctification.

20 For when you were slaves of sin, you were free in regard to righteousness.

21 Therefore what benefit were you then deriving from the things of which you are now ashamed? For the outcome of those things is death.

22 But now having been freed from sin and enslaved to God, you derive your benefit, resulting in sanctification, and the outcome, eternal life.

23 For the wages of sin is death, but the free gift of God is eternal life in Christ Jesus our Lord.

Mark the following words in a distinctive way:

a. **sin**

b. **die(d), dead, death**

c. **slave(s), enslaved**

d. **free(d)**

e. **reign**

f. **life, live(s)**

g. **obey, obedience**

When you finish marking these words, that is all you need to do for today. (By the way, have I told you how I rejoice over your diligence in studying God's Word this way? I know it will not leave you the same person. The change will be for the better, precious one, if you will live in the light of what you learn from God's Word.)

DAY FOUR

Today I want you to continue to observe Romans 6 so that you will see for yourself exactly what God is saying.

I could simply explain it all to you, but how would you know if what I was saying were right or wrong? You wouldn't know, unless you knew for yourself what the text said. Therefore, Beloved, although this is time-consuming labor, it will reap a wonderful, eternal harvest if you will labor diligently. "The hard-working farmer ought to be the first to receive his share of the crops. Consider what I say, for the Lord will give you understanding in everything" (II Timothy 2:6-7).

Now then, with that word of exhortation, let me give you your assignment. Take the words: **sin; die(d), dead,** or **death;** and **slave(s)** or **enslaved** that you marked in Romans 6 yesterday, and list everything you observed in the text that has to do with each. For instance, you would list everything that you observed about sin, etc.

SIN
1. We are not to continue in it.
2. We died to sin.
3. _____ .

That is your example. Now it is your turn. Write in the following space, but if you run out of space, use your notebook.

DAY FIVE

If you ever really grasp with your mind, heart, and will the truths of Romans 6, you will understand the great victory God wrought for you through Calvary. It will transform the way that you walk, for you will walk by faith even as you have been saved by faith, which is what Colossians 2:6-7 admonishes us to do.

As you read through Romans 6, you will find the word **baptism**. There is debate among theologians as to whether this refers to water baptism or our identification with Christ. At this point, I do not think it would serve our purpose to debate that issue. I could possibly lose some of you in the process, thus, missing what we need to see that will pertain to our healing from the awful soulish ravages of sin.

Whether by water or by salvation, what Paul wants us to see is our identification with the Lord Jesus Christ.

1. Read through Romans 6 again, and mark each phrase **with Christ** or **with Him** in a distinctive color or diagram.

2. Now read Romans 6:1-11. What have we been baptized or united into? Take into consideration all of the **with Christ** and **with Him** phrases you just marked. Be as specific as the text.

3. Finally, Beloved, write out what your identification with Jesus Christ has personally wrought for you.

4. Now let's spend a little time in worship. When we worship, we take a look at God's **"worth ship."** We recognize and honor Him for Who He is or what He has done. Worship is a key step in the healing process. You might want to worship Him in prayer, song, poetry—in silent meditation and reflection.

There is more that you need to see in Romans 6, but we will look at that tomorrow. You are loved.

DAY SIX

The key to living victoriously over any problem in life is in living in determined, diligent, unwavering obedience to truth, no matter how you feel, no matter what anyone else would offer that would be apart from or contrary to His Word. Mental assent does not profit anything if there is not a doing of what you know God says you are to do.

As we look at the divine process of healing our hurts, there are fundamental truths we must know and embrace. Otherwise, there can be no divine healing. Oh, we may get a psychological Band-aid. We may find a way of healing that is not from God and that may work to some degree, but the consequences of turning to the arm of flesh or to a spirit that is not from God could be deadly. The flesh produces nothing but death, and, of course, a spirit not from God can lead to demonic oppression.

Our identification with Christ in His death, burial, and resurrection is one of those fundamental truths that will bring healing of the wounds we have inflicted upon ourselves through our own sin, and it will also bring healing of the wounds that others, in rank disobedience to God, have inflicted upon us. Our identification with Christ brings newness of life. In the week to come, we are going to begin to understand some of the glorious benefits of this new life that is ours.

Now, Beloved, let's return to Romans 6, for there is yet more you need to see. Ask the Father to take the veil off of these truths and to engrave them in the fleshly tables of your heart, so that you might become, as the Scripture says, a living epistle known and read by all men (II Corinthians 3:2).

1. Take the remaining words you marked in Romans 6, and make a list of everything you learn from these key words as they relate to every child of God. The words were:

    a. **free(d)**   c. **life, live(s)**

    b. **reign**   d. **obey, obedience**

2. What are God's commands or exhortations to the believer in Romans 6? List them in the space provided.

3. In Romans 6:15-23, Paul contrasts two kinds of slaves. List them, and note what you learn from the text regarding each.

4. Which category do you fit in, Beloved? How do you know?

DAY SEVEN

Many times when a person has been deeply wounded, they feel as if they have no worth, no value as a human being. You can know with an absolute certainty that feelings or thoughts like this do not come from God if you are truly His. They have their origin in Satan, the father of lies, the accuser. As we will see later, Satan's primary target of attack is the mind. The Christian's armor, as Ephesians 6 tells us, includes the helmet of salvation.

When we understand our salvation, we see our purpose as a human being, created in His image, marred though it may be. Through salvation, the work of the Holy Spirit, and the transforming power of the Word of God, a gradual transformation will take place conforming us to the image of His Son.

In our last day of study for this week, I want you to focus on the truth of John 15:16.

1. Look up John 15:16 and write it out.

2. Now just from observing what the verse says, without reading anything into it, what do you learn about the child of God from this verse? List the facts in the space that follows.

3. Now then, Beloved, forgetting how you feel, forgetting what you think about yourself, and forgetting what anyone else has said about you, according to this verse in the Word of God, does your life as a child of God have worth and purpose?

4. Considering all that you have learned this week, write out a prayer to God. In that prayer make a commitment to live in accordance with the truth you have seen in His Word. Remember, to be a hearer of God's Word and not a doer is to delude yourself and to miss God's blessing.

WEEK
6

*God Is In Control,
And He Cares*

And we know that God causes all things to work together for good to those who love God, to those who are called according to His purpose.
Romans 8:28

DAY ONE

It's not the future that tears us up, unless, of course, we feel that our tomorrows are going to hold more of the past. From as close as yesterday back, it is the past which torments us. If we panic about the future, it is because we are dealing with fear and anxiety, which are usually provoked by experiences of the past. We fear the future may hold more of today or our yesterdays. Or if our past has not been full of trauma and yet we still fear the future, then, realize it or not, we are dealing with unreality, for we know not what the future holds. Oh, we may surmise what is ahead, and our speculations may come to pass, but as of today those speculations are yet future and their validity known with absolute certainty only to God.

If you hurt or have hurt, you know that it is the thoughts of the past that are the enemy—destroying the happiness of today and blowing threatening storm clouds of doom on what is yet to be. However, if the wounded and hurting could learn to deal with their past, if they knew how to apply God's balm of Gilead to the wounds of what has been, they would begin to experience the Lord's healing of their hurts.

Are you wounded, Beloved, hurting because of your past? There is hope; there is healing. If you will but cry, "Heal me, O Lord," and then believe what God's Word says and live accordingly moment by moment, you will be healed.

Let me have the privilege of taking you through the process of dealing with the traumas of your past and showing you how to apply the balm of Gilead.

Last week you saw two key truths that are vital in dealing with the past. Let me review these, and then we will move on. First, you saw that when you receive the Lord Jesus Christ, when you believe in His death, burial, and resurrection as God's only means of taking care of your sin and giving you the free gift of eternal life, you are identified in Jesus's death and resurrection. It is this identification that takes care of sin, setting you free from slavery to sin, so that you can be a slave of righteousness.

Secondly, you also saw from John 15:16 that your salvation was initiated by God. Mystery though it may be, hard to comprehend with our finite minds, God does the choosing. We didn't choose Him; He chose us. And when He chose us, it was not without purpose. God ordained that we should go and, in the going, that we would bear fruit, and the fruit that we would bear would not be temporal, but abiding. Not only that, but we would also have access to our God through the name of Jesus Christ, for whatever we asked in His name, Jesus promised to do it.

The bottom line of these two truths is that you, being set free from slavery to sin, now have a purpose in life. Your life has eternal value, not because of anything you are or that you did, but because God in His wondrous grace chose you to be His forever.

Now, your question probably is… "But what about my past? It has so traumatized me that I will never be profitable to anyone!"

That, Beloved, is what you may think, but I can tell you that it is not biblical thinking. Aren't you glad?

You have one, and only one, assignment for today. Pray that God will take the veil off of your eyes and show you how He, the Great Redeemer, can redeem the seemingly destructive traumas of the past and use them for your good and His glory. Write out your prayer in the provided space.

DAY TWO

Romans 8:28 is a Scripture that is familiar to so many Christians, and yet I wonder if it is a verse that we quote glibly without ever really comprehending the depth of its meaning and the context in which it is given.

Your assignment for today, Beloved, is an easy one, and yet it can pack a spiritual wallop that can knock you into the arms of the Prince of Peace. I know, because it is a verse that God has used to take me through one of the greatest traumas of my life. I am not at liberty to share what the trauma is because of the cause of the trauma. However, to save your curiosity, let me just say that it has nothing to do with my precious husband or with our relationship. Simply know that I would share it if I could, if it would help you, but I cannot because it might hurt another. I simply want you to know that I live by what I am about to share with you over the next few weeks.

Printed out for you is Romans 8:28-39. Read it carefully. Mark the following key words in a distinctive way: **God, Christ** or **Christ Jesus,** and all pronouns referring to the Godhead. Also, mark every personal pronoun referring to the child of God **(us, we, whom, those, these)**. When you finish marking your key words, list below the passage everything you learn about God and about Jesus Christ. Please do not do anything more than this today.

ROMANS 8:28-39

28 And we know that God causes all things to work

together for good to those who love God, to those who

are called according to His purpose.

29 For whom He foreknew, He also predestined to

become conformed to the image of His Son, that He might

be the first-born among many brethren;

30 and whom He predestined, these He also called; and whom He called, these He also justified; and whom He justified, these He also glorified.

31 What then shall we say to these things? If God is for us, who is against us?

32 He who did not spare His own Son, but delivered Him up for us all, how will He not also with Him freely give us all things?

33 Who will bring a charge against God's elect? God is the one who justifies;

34 who is the one who condemns? Christ Jesus is He who died, yes, rather who was raised, who is at the right hand of God, who also intercedes for us.

35 Who shall separate us from the love of Christ? Shall tribulation, or distress, or persecution, or famine, or nakedness, or peril, or sword?

36 Just as it is written, ''For Thy sake we are being put to death all day long; we were considered as sheep to be slaughtered.''

37 But in all these things we overwhelmingly conquer through Him who loved us.

38 For I am convinced that neither death, nor life, nor angels, nor principalities, nor things

present, nor things to come, nor powers,

39 nor height, nor depth, nor any other

created thing, shall be able to separate us from the

love of God, which is in Christ Jesus our Lord.

DAY THREE

So often we quote or read Romans 8:28, and we stop there. Although a period comes after verse 28 in our Bible, still the thought continues. Our question should be, "How does everything work together for good for those who love God, for those who are the called according to His purpose?" What is the good that "everything" is going to accomplish?

You can answer that question for yourself simply by observing the text of Romans 8:28-39. There are other Scriptures we need to consider with our passage in Romans 8, but these will come later. Today, your assignment is as follows:

1. Read through the passage from Romans 8 that you marked yesterday.

2. In the right hand margin, list everything you observed as a result of marking the personal pronouns which refer to the child of God. These, Beloved, are truths which belong to you, if you belong to Him. And if you do not belong to Him yet, you can know, Beloved, that God wants you to come to Him for your salvation and adoption into His family.

3. When you finish with your list, write out below the good that God intends to accomplish in your life through everything that has happened to you. (If you are hurting terribly, or if there is a great deal of bitterness and unforgiveness in your heart, then, Beloved, this assignment may be hard to do at this point. I understand. Do the best you can—give it a good try. In several weeks, we will deal with bitterness and unforgiveness. Wait patiently. How healing it will be!)

4. What questions are provoked in your mind or your heart by Romans 8:28-39? List them in the space that follows. (For example: "How could the abuse, the incest I have endured work together for good?" [Let me remind you again that in the weeks to come you'll begin to see the answers to these questions.])

DAY FOUR

One of the questions that I think Romans 8:28 would provoke in your mind is, "What does the 'all things' include? Does it mean 'all things' since I became a Christian, or does it mean 'all things' including the past?" I believe the answer to the two questions which I just posed is absolutely critical to your healing. I know that it has been to mine as regards my past and its effect not only on my own life, but also on the lives of my sons whom I love dearly.

Last week you saw that you were chosen by God. If you could learn when you were chosen by God, then you would know what time frame "all things" covers. Since it is the past that troubles us the most, we need to know if "all things" covers the past, and, if so, how far back. There are several passages which I believe will show us that "all things" includes the past. We will look at these Scriptures later. For this week, it will help if we can look at several other points before we leave Romans 8.

God's purpose for every believer is transformation into the image of Jesus Christ. Romans 8:29 tells us that God foreknew us and in knowing us beforehand He predestined, or marked out before, that we should be conformed to the image of His Son. Conformation to the image of Jesus Christ is achieved through our proper relationship to God, through our response to the Word of God, and through the suffering which attends the life of every child of God. This will be our topic of study for the remainder of the week.

First, let's take a look at how Christlikeness, or conformation to the image of Jesus Christ, comes through the Word of God. Take a minute to read II Corinthians 3. In this chapter, Paul is contrasting the Old Covenant, the Law put on tables of stone, and the New Covenant of Grace, which is written upon our hearts by the indwelling Holy Spirit.

In II Corinthians 3, Paul explains that when a person comes to Jesus Christ a veil is taken away. This is the veil of the Old Covenant, a covenant which the Jews misunderstood and, in their misunderstanding, thought was the means of their salvation. They thought that they could be saved by the keeping of the Law. Although salvation had always been by grace, the Jews misunderstood the purpose of the Law and felt that somehow, by its keeping, they could make themselves acceptable to God. "For not knowing about God's righteousness, and seeking to establish their own, they did not subject themselves to the righteousness of God" (Romans 10:3). They sought a righteousness by works, and, in doing so, they proved that they did not understand their total poverty of spirit when it came to their ability to be righteous. The Jews could not see that God "saved us, not on the basis of deeds which we have done in righteousness, but according to His mercy, by the washing of regeneration and renewing by the Holy Spirit, whom He poured out upon us richly through Jesus Christ our Savior, that being justified by His grace we might be made heirs according to the hope of eternal life" (Titus 3:5-7). O Beloved, you aren't blinded as the Jews were, are you? There is not a veil over your eyes that causes you to think that you can attain salvation and peace with God through your own works or by the keeping of God's Law, is there? If, in any way, you think you have earned or even merit salvation, then, my friend, you are blind to truth. There is a veil there, and it will only disappear when you trust in Jesus alone to save you.

When a person understands and accepts that salvation is by pure grace—unearned, unmerited favor—bestowed upon man because of what Jesus Christ accomplished as the God-man at Calvary, then the veil is taken away. Faith in the grace of God brings a person into the kingdom of God. Man is saved from the penalty of sin, which is death. However, salvation does not stop there. God not only saves you, but He begins the process of transforming you into the image He intended for man when He created Adam and Eve. That image is man unmarred by sin. That image is the image of Jesus Christ. And how is that image achieved in you and me, who once lived in sin? It begins at salvation with the indwelling of the Holy Spirit and is continued through the transformation which comes through the cleansing power of the Word of God.

Look up the following verses, and write out what they say. Watch for words that refer to cleansing or transformation. By the way, the Greek word for **transformation** is *metamorphoo*. Interesting, isn't it, when you stop and think about the metamorphosis that takes place when a caterpillar is changed into a butterfly!

1. II Corinthians 3:18

2. Romans 12:2

3. Ephesians 5:25-27 (Watch carefully what Christ does for the church. Note the **how** and **why** of it all.)

Well, my precious student, that is enough for today. Tomorrow we will take a look at how suffering is used of God to transform us into the image of His Son.

DAY FIVE

As I said yesterday, suffering is one of God's primary means of conforming us to the image of His Son, Jesus Christ. As the God-man, Jesus suffered. As a man or woman whom God wants to conform to the image of God, you and I must suffer.

The author of Hebrews writes of Jesus: "Although He was a Son, He learned obedience from the things which He suffered" (Hebrews 5:8). Philippians 1:29 states, "For to you it has been granted for Christ's sake, not only to believe in Him, but also to suffer for His sake." Romans 8:16-18 assures us that "the Spirit Himself bears witness with our spirit that we are children of God, and if children, heirs also, heirs of God and fellow heirs with Christ, if indeed we suffer with Him in order that we may also be glorified with Him. For I consider that the sufferings of this present time are not worthy to be compared with the glory that is to be revealed to us."

Suffering is often likened in Scripture to the refining of gold or silver. We see this in I Peter 1:6-7: "In this you greatly rejoice, even though now for a little while, if necessary, you have been distressed by various trials, that the proof of your faith, being more precious than gold which is perishable, even though tested by fire, may be found to result in praise and glory and honor at the revelation of Jesus Christ."

When silver or gold is mined from the earth, there are other metals or impurities mixed or alloyed with it. For the gold or silver to be pure, the impurities have to go. So it is with you and me. For us to become conformed to the image of Jesus Christ, our impurities have to go! In the Book of Jeremiah, you will find reference to God purifying His people even as silver is purified in a furnace of fire. To get rid of impurities or dross, as God calls it, silver was melted in a series of fires which would release the dross and, thus, would allow the dross to rise to the top of the crucible where it could be removed by the silversmith.

Suffering provides the fire by which God purifies His children. As we saw in Hebrews 5:8, suffering is God's means of teaching us obedience. The question that confronts us then is, "How will you respond to suffering?" Not only the suffering which awaits you, but also to the suffering which you have endured in the past? Will you let it embitter you or transform you? Will you hold onto the dross, or will you be made like Jesus?

Every trial of life, Beloved, is a test of your faith, for with each trial you are called upon to make a decision. The decision is: Will you believe God and, thus, respond in the way God says respond; or will you cling to the dross of independent disobedience and, therefore, sin in the unbelief of the flesh?

Let me take you, for a brief moment, to II Corinthians 4, for there are some precious truths there that will help you deal with and handle suffering. Listen to the Word of God: "But we have this treasure (speaking of the indwelling of the Spirit through the New Covenant) in earthen vessels, that the surpassing greatness of the power may be of God and not from ourselves; we are afflicted in every way, but not crushed; perplexed, but not despairing; persecuted, but not forsaken; struck down, but not destroyed; always carrying about in the body the dying of Jesus, that the life of Jesus also may be manifested in our body. For we who live are constantly being delivered over to death for Jesus' sake, that the life of Jesus also may be manifested in our mortal flesh. So death works in us, but life in you" (4:7-12).

O Beloved, as you read this passage, can you see how God can use all that you endure or have endured to give hope and life to others? Can you see how, if you will believe God, trust Him, and cling to Him in faith, your obedience can be used to minister life to others?

And how are you going to walk in such a way as to live this out? Paul goes on to tell you in II Corinthians 4:16-18.

1. Look up II Corinthians 4:16-18, and write it out.

2. In your own words, write out what you must do if you are going to walk in faith's victory.

Think about these things, for your healing is dependent upon your response. I say all of this neither to discourage you...nor to cause you to throw this book across the room in anger, because, at this point, you may not think you can handle what I am saying.

Be patient, Beloved. Don't walk away. We have progressed this far. Finish the course you have begun. Don't let the one who would destroy you hold you captive. Remember the devil is a liar and a murderer (John 8:44) who would keep you from your Great Physician and His healing balm.

DAY SIX

Suffering can refine us and conform us into the image of God, or it can embitter and harden our hearts, keeping us from Christlikeness. We decide or choose by our response of belief or unbelief.

To some, suffering is a sign that God does not care about them or that He has abandoned them. Their suffering embitters them. I will never forget a woman with whom I shared the gospel. Oh, how she was hurting...and I hurt with her when I heard her story. I met her when I was out doing door-to-door evangelism with some people from our church. As we sat in her living room talking, I could not help but notice the lines on her face that belied her age, making her appear older than she was. Her life seemed in as much disarray as her home. Hopelessness hung in the air. As I shared the gospel, telling her of her need of the Savior and the love of God, her words lunged at me, going for my spiritual jugular vein, "When God gives me back my baby, then I'll listen to Him." The presentation of the gospel came to a halt as I probed to try and find out what she meant when she made that statement. Her baby had died in a fire. I was about a year old in Christ when this happened. I didn't know what I know now, or I would have dealt with her differently. I would have more wisely and gently tried to dress her excruciatingly painful wound with the balm of Gilead. All I can do is trust God that if she ever would have listened then someone else would have been sent by Him to minister to her. I did not see her come to Christ. She refused to believe that, although God would not give her back her baby, He could someday allow her to live forever with Him and her baby. At that time, her bitterness had hardened her heart, and she missed the healing that God alone could bring. A bitter woman saw me to the door.

According to Romans 8:35-39, nothing can separate us from the love of God. The tribulations, distresses, and persecutions that come into our lives are not meant to destroy us but to drive us into His everlasting arms of love. In His sovereignty, God has allowed suffering. The One Who sits upon the Throne of thrones, reigning supremely, doing according to His will in the army of heaven and among the inhabitants of the earth, has you in His omnipotent hands. And because God is love and because He loves you with an everlasting love, then everything that comes into your life must be filtered through His fingers of love. No one can touch you, speak to you, look at you, or do anything to you without His permission. If adversity comes into your life, it comes with His permission. And if it comes, it will work together for your good. It will be used to conform you into His image. It will not keep you from the kingdom of heaven, for "whom He predestined, these He also called; and whom He called, these He also justified; and whom He justified, these He also glorified....Who shall separate us from the love of Christ? Shall tribulation, or distress, or persecution, or famine, or nakedness, or peril, or sword? Just as it is written, 'For Thy sake we are being put to death all day long; we were considered as sheep to be slaughtered.' But in all these things we overwhelmingly conquer through Him who loved us. For I am convinced that neither death, nor life, nor angels, nor principalities, nor things present, nor things to come, nor powers, nor height, nor depth, nor any other created thing, shall be able to separate us from the love of God, which is in Christ Jesus our Lord" (Romans 8:30, 35-39).

Whatever God allows to come into your life, Beloved, you can know it is not designed to embitter, disfigure, or destroy you; rather, it is permitted by a loving God for the purpose of conforming you into the image of His Son, Jesus Christ.

Believest, thou, this? For further proof, look up the following verses of Scripture, and write them out. Then meditate upon them.

1. Write out the last three words of I John 4:8. This is an unchanging attribute of God. Therefore, He will never act apart from what you learn about Him from this verse.

2. Daniel 4:34-35

3. Isaiah 45:5-7 (The word **evil** [KJV] or **calamity** [NASB] means "adversity.")

4. Psalm 103:19

5. Deuteronomy 32:39

6. Jeremiah 29:11 (What God says of Israel, His chosen people, I believe He says of you, His chosen.)

How I pray, Beloved, that you will believe Him, and that you will know His heart towards you.

DAY SEVEN

As we have studied thus far, we have seen that God, in His sovereignty, chose us, ordained that we should go and bear fruit, and promised us that all things in our lives would work together for good and would be used to conform us to the image of His Son.

In our final and brief day of study for this week, I want us to look at when we were chosen by God and also to look at what, if anything, caused God to choose us.

1. Read Romans 8:29. According to this verse, for what did God predestine us?

2. Now read Ephesians 1:3-6. It is printed out for you here.

EPHESIANS 1:3-6

3 Blessed be the God and Father of our Lord Jesus Christ, who has blessed us with every spiritual blessing in the heavenly places in Christ,

4 just as He chose us in Him before the foundation of the world, that we should be holy and blameless before Him. In love

5 He predestined us to adoption as sons through Jesus Christ to Himself, according to the kind intention of His will,

6 to the praise of the glory of His grace, which He freely bestowed on us in the Beloved.

3. Whenever you read the Word, you always ought to ask yourself the ''5 W's and an H'': **who, what, when, where, why,** and **how.** Therefore, to help you get into practice, ask and answer the ''5 W's and an H'' concerning these verses. Examine them from every possible angle. Ask: Who was speaking? To whom? Who blessed? Who chose? Cover each ''W'' and every ''H'' you can in these verses. Write out your insights. If you need more space, use an extra piece of paper.

4. Now in a single sentence, summarize what you learn regarding when God chose you and what His purpose was.

5. Finally, Beloved, how does what you have seen today relate to your past and to what you learned from Romans 8:28-39? If you do not see any relationship, then be honest...but do not give up.

There is yet much more for us to see on this subject of dealing with our past, and I believe the Lord will greatly use the truths that we will see in the coming week to minister healing to you in a very special way. Or, as I have been saying, if you don't need healing, I know God will use these truths to help you minister to your mate, your family, or to others.

My prayer for you, beloved and diligent student, is that God will show you how precious you are in His sight, not because of who or what you are, but simply because of Who He is and because of the unmerited favor He has chosen to bestow in the riches of His glory upon you as a vessel of His mercy.

WEEK
7

God Is There!!

Behold, I have inscribed you
on the palms of My hands.
Isaiah 49:16

DAY ONE

There are many who, like me, have hurt because of the self-inflicted wounds that have come from living in open rebellion to the clear commandments of God. Instead of allowing the Law of God to keep them from a life of overt sin until they came to faith in Jesus Christ, they shook their fist rebelliously in the face of God and went out and did their own thing! And what an awful harvest they reaped! A harvest, as Romans 6 says, of which they are ashamed once they come to know the Lord Jesus Christ.

Instead of rejoicing over God's forgiveness and trusting that even their wretched life of sin can be redeemed and be used in some way for His glory, they weep and live with "if onlys." Although Jesus Christ paid for their sin at Calvary, putting it behind His back and remembering it no more, they keep it ever before their eyes.

The memory of their sin is worn like a black shroud of mourning, keeping others from beholding the radiance that His forgiveness should bring. Grief over past sins saps their strength, leaving them weak and even impotent in serving God. They need to hear or be reminded of God's word through Nehemiah to men who, like them, had sinned, "Do not be grieved, for the joy of the LORD is your strength" (8:10).

Is there any cure for those who are saved and yet who are haunted by ghosts of past sins? Is there any balm for those who know that their sins are forgiven, but who still have a hard time seeing how God can use them because they feel like a second-class citizen in the kingdom of God? Yes, there is, Beloved. Let's look at it.

1. For the sake of review, go back and read Ephesians 1:3-6. You might also want to review the "5 W's and an H" which you observed when you studied these verses last week.

2. Now then, I want us to take a look at Galatians 1:11-17, where Paul refers briefly to his conversion. Read this passage carefully, and then write out what you learn about the timing of Paul's salvation.

3. How could what you have learned today regarding the time of salvation help a person deal with the trauma of their past? Be as specific as you can in your answer.

DAY TWO

I remember how I used to ache over my past, groaning in my inner man, because I had not come to know Jesus Christ earlier in life. I thought of what might have been had I heard the gospel before I ever divorced Tom. I thought of what could have been for my children had I not gone into a life of flagrant sin and immorality. I lived with ghosts of "if only," and I was miserable. And then through the wonderful, transforming power of the Word of God, I was set free. As I literally immersed myself in the Bible, I saw that God saved me when it pleased Him. I saw that in the sovereignty of God I was chosen in Christ Jesus before the foundation of the world to be adopted as His child; but I also saw that in the sovereignty of God the timing of my salvation was God's doing. In God's sovereignty, I would not be saved until I was twenty-nine—already divorced and caught in the snare of immorality. God knew that, and, in His sovereignty, He planned that even the timing of my salvation would work together for good.

How utterly, totally, absolutely, incredibly awesome this was to me! And how I love to share these truths with others and watch God use what He taught me in my pain of ignorance to minister to others who need the same healing that I needed.

I have a note written to me on lined paper. The side of the paper with the three holes is ragged and fringed where it was hastily torn from a three-ringed notebook on January 17, 1986. I treasure the note. It is a testimony to the healing power of the balm of Gilead. It's an answer to the cry, "Lord, heal my hurts."

Let me share it with you, Beloved, just as it was written but leaving out some references to time, and then we will call it a day.

"Your teaching tonight has so freed me to believe that God has chosen me from before there was time to be His—knowing full well that my life would be so full of sin.

"Before I was saved, I was an adulteress, stole the man who lived next door to my parents from his wife and children, had his child out of wedlock and finally succeeded in getting him to marry me when our child was ___ years old. When I came to the Lord, I was devastated to realize what pain and suffering my sin caused so many, but especially how I had grieved my Lord. God has redeemed so much of the hurt to so many and in His miraculous ways has brought us to a place of loving one another, but I still have felt that He let me slip in the back door and that never could I be truly special to Him.

"But, oh Kay, I know that He chose me with full knowledge of how wretched I would be and that I am now called holy and blameless by the blood of my precious Jesus.

"I can scarcely take it in. How grateful I am to my God. How I want Him to receive all of me to be used for His glory and purpose.

"I have never done Precept before, but in two days I have become totally committed to know God by His Word. How I want to know truth, to stand on truth and to spread His truth."

Here, Beloved, is the testimony of a woman who has come to know the truth, and, in the knowing, to be set free. Free because she believed God! O Beloved, are you believing God?

DAY THREE

I realize that it is one thing to deal with a past that has been traumatized through one's self-inflicted wounds of sin, but what about living with a past that has been traumatized by others? What about those who have been mentally, emotionally, physically, or sexually abused by others...or by their parents, or by those whom they at one time trusted? Is there any real, genuine, lasting healing for them?

Or what about those who are hurting because they are bitter and angry because physically they do not like themselves? Or who, because of physical infirmities or propensities such as being overweight, have suffered rejection that might have come in a dozen different but painfully real forms? Is there any healing for them?

What about those who are bulimic or anorexic? Can God's Word cure them ...or does psychology or psychiatry hold the answer?

Can the Word of God heal those molested by perverted, twisted, ungodly sinners?

Yes, yes, yes!

If you are going to say, "No, the Bible only deals with the spiritual. These are psychological needs which need professional help," then you must also say that God could do nothing apart from the advent of psychology around one hundred years ago. You would have to say that the Word of God was impotent under the ministry of the Holy Spirit. And, in the saying of this, you would elevate man to omniscience and omnipotence. You would delay man's healing until man finally evolved to such a state, where in his own wisdom, he could gain insight into the intricacies of the soul of man. And then, I would have to ask, "Does psychology or psychiatry really effect a permanent cure apart from God?"

Can any real, Bible-believing child of God say that God cannot heal apart from psychology...or that He even needs psychology? I cannot see how such a statement is possible if one holds to the whole counsel of God as laid down from Genesis to Revelation? Can we question whether or not the Bible has the answers for any and every situation of life—even the traumas which have come from the hands of ungodly sinners? I honestly don't believe we can and still maintain a faith pleasing to God. For "without faith it is impossible to please Him, for he who comes to God must believe that He is, and that He is a rewarder of those who seek Him" (Hebrews 11:6). God is Jehovah-rapha, the God Who heals.

And since it is God Who heals through the balm of the Word, where does one begin the healing process? Well, obviously I believe a good place to begin is where I am beginning—with an understanding of the character and sovereignty of God. However, it does not end there. I believe the reason so many are not healed when they could be is because they do not have an understanding of the attending care of God in bringing us to salvation. Nor do they understand how thoroughly and completely God saved us. Therefore, spiritually they resemble street people picking up the world's trash in order to sustain life, when they could be dwelling before the Throne of truth, living as more than conquerors.

Tomorrow we will begin soaking up the truths of Psalm 139, a Psalm which will explain God's attending care and, in the process, give us gems of truth which will help us deal with the traumas of the past. However, as we look at this Psalm, I do not want you to think that this is all we are going to say regarding dealing with the traumas of incest, rape, rejection, and other heinous sins inflicted by others. This is just the beginning of a string of Scriptures that will heal your wounds, making of them pearls of great beauty which will adorn you in Christlikeness. All that you are learning is part of a healing process that is being effected precept upon precept, truth upon truth, so remember, "Hangeth, thou, in there."

Just keep crying out in faith, "Heal me, O Lord, and I will be healed," and know that whatever you ask in His name, He will do. What better prayer could you pray in the name of your Jehovah-rapha than this?!

Speaking of our need to pray for healing, I think it would be profitable for you to look up Luke 11:1-13, read it carefully, and answer the following questions:

1. What is the main theme of this passage? Or to put it another way, what is the main thing Jesus is dealing with in these verses?

2. What is the point Jesus is making regarding this theme in verses 5-10? (Hint: **Ask, seek,** and **knock** are all in the present tense in the Greek, which denotes continuous or habitual action.)

3. What is the point Jesus is making in verses 11-13?

4. What can you learn from these verses about praying for healing?

DAY FOUR

As I said yesterday, one of the key passages to be applied as His balm for healing the traumas of the past is Psalm 139. This Psalm is printed out for you. Your assignment for today is twofold. As a loving teacher, may I urge you to do your assignment exactly as you are instructed to do? Don't skip over anything, for there is a purpose in it all.

1. Read through Psalm 139. Read it aloud, and read it slowly. Concentrate on what you are reading, on what the psalmist is saying. Do this at least three times—aloud each time. When you read something aloud repeatedly, you will find yourself automatically memorizing it. There is something about the speaking and hearing of it that causes your mind to retain it.

2. Read through the Psalm a fourth time. This time mark each use of the words **Thou** and **Thee**. Then at the end of today's assignment, list everything you learn from the use of **Thou** and **Thee**.

PSALM 139

1 O LORD, Thou hast searched me and known me.

2 Thou dost know when I sit down and when I rise up; Thou dost understand my thought from afar.

3 Thou dost scrutinize my path and my lying down, and art intimately acquainted with all my ways.

4 Even before there is a word on my tongue, behold, O LORD, Thou dost know it all.

5 Thou hast enclosed me behind and before, and laid Thy hand upon me.

6 Such knowledge is too wonderful for me; it is too high, I cannot attain to it.

7 Where can I go from Thy Spirit? Or where can I flee from Thy presence?

8 If I ascend to heaven, Thou art there; if I make my bed in Sheol, behold, Thou art there.

9 If I take the wings of the dawn, if I dwell in the remotest part of the sea,

10 Even there Thy hand will lead me, and Thy right hand will lay hold of me.

11 If I say, "Surely the darkness will overwhelm me, and the light around me will be night,"

12 Even the darkness is not dark to Thee, and the night is as bright as the day. Darkness and light are alike to Thee.

13 For Thou didst form my inward parts; Thou didst weave me in my mother's womb.

14 I will give thanks to Thee, for I am fearfully and wonderfully made; wonderful are Thy works, and my soul knows it very well.

15 My frame was not hidden from Thee, when I was made in secret, and skillfully wrought in the depths of the earth.

16 Thine eyes have seen my unformed substance; and in Thy book they were all written, the days that were ordained for me, when as yet there was not one of them.

17 How precious also are Thy thoughts to me, O God! How vast is the sum of them!

18 If I should count them, they would outnumber the sand. When I awake, I am still with Thee.

19 O that Thou wouldst slay the wicked, O God; depart from me, therefore, men of bloodshed.

20 For they speak against Thee wickedly, and Thine enemies take Thy name in vain.

21 Do I not hate those who hate Thee, O LORD? And do I not loathe those who rise up against Thee?

22 I hate them with the utmost hatred; they have become my enemies.

23 Search me, O God, and know my heart; try me and know my anxious thoughts;

24 And see if there be any hurtful way in me, and lead me in the everlasting way.

DAY FIVE

Once again we are going to spend the day in Psalm 139. As a matter of fact, Beloved, Psalm 139 is going to be our focus for the remainder of this week.

If you will carefully and diligently do all that I feel God has laid upon my heart for you to do, I believe that your relationship with the Father will take on a new depth of intimacy and understanding. Therefore, I am not going to be writing or sharing much with you, because you need to give your time and energies in study of the Psalm itself. (In my audio and/or video teaching tapes, I will take you through the Psalm verse by verse, should you desire to listen.)

1. Read through Psalm 139 again, and mark each use of the words **Thy** and **Thine,** and then list what **Thy** and **Thine** modify (e.g., Spirit, hand, etc.). Record what you learn about each "Thy_____" and how it personally relates to you.

2. Now then, read through Psalm 139 aloud again three times. Do not let your mind wander as you read. Ask God to speak to you by opening the eyes of your understanding, so that you might plumb the depths of the truths captured in this Psalm.

DAY SIX

In Psalm 139, God wonderfully reveals different aspects of His character, nature, or attributes. I want you to see these on your own before I share them with you. Therefore, before you read any further, Beloved, would you list what you learn about God from this Psalm? You might write out your insights as if you were describing what you have learned about God in this Psalm to someone else.

At the end of this book you will find a listing of the attributes of God. Read through them carefully. As you come across an attribute of God which is revealed in this Psalm, record it, along with the verse in which you saw this attribute.

Now then, Beloved, returning to the list of God's attributes at the end of this book, is there anything you learned about God today that you feel could or would help you deal with the hurts which you have endured? If so, write it out.

As one reads Psalm 139, not only is there much which is revealed about God, but there is much to be learned about oneself. Read through the Psalm again, and this time draw a little stick figure over every reference to **I, me, my**. When you finish, note all that you learn from these personal pronouns. As you write down your insights, put a star beside those which you can personalize since they are true for every child of God as well as for the psalmist who wrote them. Put a question mark beside those truths which you must determine will either be embraced as yours or not.

Now then, Beloved, I want to talk with those of you who are disappointed in your parents, those of you who are hurting because of what your father or mother has done to you, or because of what they have failed to be to you. I want to ask you two questions:

1. Who allowed you to have the parents that you have?

2. If your parents have failed you, if they have not been the kind of parents God wanted them to be, what must you assume in the light of all that you have been learning from the Bible?

Think on these things, and we will deal with them in the weeks to come. Tomorrow we will look at a summary of Psalm 139.

DAY SEVEN

In the Book of Psalms, Psalm 139 is like the spine-thrilling clanging of cymbals, as man's consciousness of God's all-encompassing love and care are recognized and verbalized. How it is my prayer, Beloved, that this Psalm will be to you a true balm of Gilead as you become aware of God's sovereign watch care over you, not only all the days of your life, but before you were even formed in your mother's womb.

Psalm 139 falls into four sections comprised of six verses each. From the perspective of focusing on God's sovereign love and care, Psalm 139 might be outlined as follows:

THE SOVEREIGN LOVE AND CARE OF GOD AS:
Verses 1-6	The Omniscient One
Verses 7-12	The Omnipresent One
Verses 13-18	The Creator-Sustainer
Verses 19-24	The Righteous Judge

How comforting it is to know that because God is omniscient, or all-knowing, He is intimately acquainted with all of your ways. I am sure as you studied this Psalm yourself that you noticed how the psalmist kept saying, "Thou, Thou, Thou." He is a God Who knows, Who understands, and, thus, Who has enclosed you behind and before. He is not a God far-off in heaven, unconcerned, unaware of the events of your life, nor of the utmost secrets of your thoughts! No, Beloved, He cares for you in such a way that He, God Himself, has laid His hand upon you! It is astounding, isn't it, that you would be the object of concern to Almighty Elohim?! As Isaiah 49:16 says, "Behold, I have inscribed you on the palms of My hands." That truth, Beloved, is born out in the nail prints on the hands of His Son!

In all of this, Beloved, you can know that there is not anything, which has been done to you, that your Father God does not know about. And remember, He is the righteous Judge, as we have seen in the outline of this Psalm. Not only does God know all about you and about what has been done to you and how you have responded, but He was also there. You were never alone. Whether you knew or recognized His presence, He was there, for there is no fleeing from His presence. He was there, my friend, even when the darkness of trauma threatened to overwhelm you. When you felt as the psalmist, "Surely the darkness will overwhelm me, and the light around me will be night," He was there protecting, keeping, preserving. Since the word for **overwhelm** in verse 11 could be translated "bruise," I think God wants us to see that, although we think the darkness—the unknown, hidden assaults of life—will bruise us forever, they can't, for He was there once again with His protective hand upon us.

Your God is not a Creator Who has brought you into existence only to abandon you. He is your Creator-Sustainer. You may have spent a great deal of time wishing that you had different parents, wondering what it would have been like had you had a mother and dad like whomever, but, Beloved, that is wasted thinking which will only make you more miserable. As you see in verses 13-16, God gave you your parents. I know that if you have had poor excuses for parents this fact may at first make you very angry with God. But, dear one, let that anger fade in the light of Romans 8:28 and I Corinthians 10:13. Your parents are not more than you can bear, although you may feel that they are. God has provided a way of escape, and, with respect to the hurts you have borne from others, I know your way of escape is by clinging in faith to the knowledge of your God and His Word. God is sufficient for all of your hurts, and He will cause your childhood to work together for your eternal good and His glory. Believe it, Beloved. Believe it, and you will find the soothing balm of Gilead healing your wounds.

God has preserved your life and brought you to this point and to this study. He has ordained the number of days you are to live when as yet there was not one of them (verse 16), and He has ordained that you know these truths regarding His sovereign love and care. Yours is to believe. He has said it all in His Word, done it all in confronting you with His truth. Now you determine your healing. The balm is there. Will you apply it? Will you cry, "Heal me, O Lord, and I will be healed. Save me, O Lord, and I will be saved"? Oh, I plead with you, to say, "Yes"!

There is one more truth I want to share regarding God as your Creator-Sustainer. You may not like the way you look physically, but God has a purpose even in that! He says that you are "fearfully and wonderfully made." You may despise yourself simply because, in one way or another, you are not built in the proportion you think you ought to be, or the design you would prefer, but even that has a purpose. Your frame was not hidden from God when you were skillfully wrought! His thoughts toward you are precious! You may believe it or not, but God does not lie! This is what He says, for all Scripture is God-breathed!

Finally in the last section of Psalm 139, we see God as the Righteous Judge. Righteous He is, for that is His character. Righteous He is able to be, because He is omniscient and omnipresent. He is all-knowing. Nothing has been hidden from Him. He will deal with the wicked. God does not expect you to side with wickedness. Nor does He want you to keep company with the wicked, with those who hate Him. His enemies are to be yours, in a sense. And yet, you are to treat His enemies and yours the way He says to treat them. You will find your instructions in the New Testament, in places such as Matthew 5:44-48 and Romans 12:14-21. (I would like you to look up those verses if you have the time, for they are so vital. Yet, I know today is very long as far as reading. I will leave you some space, just in case you want to write down the essence of these verses.)

What I want you to see is that you do not have to deal out retribution to your enemies. God will righteously judge those who have hurt you. Your enemies are His. Therefore, my friend, you must let God deal with them. That is not for you to do. As you will see later, God calls you to forgive your enemies. It is unforgiveness that can even keep you from the kingdom of heaven.

Your responsibility is also to let God keep your heart pure by searching it and letting you know your anxious thoughts. He is the One Who will show you any hurtful ways in your life, so that you might deal with them and walk in His everlasting way. Isn't it wonderful to know that your Father will keep you pure for the asking?!!

Well, Beloved, I could go on and on, but I know this is getting very long for a day's study. Therefore, let me close with the following word of exhortation. In the light of all of the infallible truths of Psalm 139, Beloved, won't you bow your knee in humble submission to the will of God and His sovereign ways, and "in everything give thanks; for this is God's will for you in Christ Jesus" (I Thessalonians 5:18)? If you will, and if you will continue to walk in faithful obedience, you will find God's divine healing.

WEEK
8

*Letting Your Mind
Be Renewed*

Therefore if any man is in Christ,
he is a new creature;
the old things passed away;
behold, new things have come.
II Corinthians 5:17

DAY ONE

As we begin our eighth week of study, let me ask you a question, Beloved. Have you ever stopped to think of how God could use the hurts you have suffered, the wounds you have endured, the rejection you have experienced, to minister to others?

As I told you last week, there was a time in my young walk with the Lord when I became depressed over my past. My mind became the hunting ground of the enemy as he continually brought before me the "what-might-have-beens" had things been different in my life. Like so many others, not only women but men also, I had my dreams and expectations of what life should be all about. In my dreams, there was peace, love, security—a picture of a wonderfully romantic marriage, a happy "Father Knows Best" or "Cosby" type of family life. Trials? Yes. But tragedies? NO! And as these thoughts of what-might-have-been or what-could-have-been-if-only cried out for my undivided attention and sympathy, I found my emotions taking a tailspin, careening seemingly out of control, doomed to crash, leaving me shattered, scattered, depressed. The past and what might have been tormented me and made my days difficult to cope with. The future could hold nothing, for it was consumed with regrets from the past.

Can you relate, my friend? Have you ever been taken captive with similar thoughts? It's a little bit of hell, isn't it? You look at those who seem to have what you have been deprived of, and you feel as if life, or even God, has maliciously cheated you of happiness. You look at those who failed you, and you know your relationship with them is not what it should be or could be. Sometimes you are torn with a dichotomy of feelings towards them—wanting their love and approval, but then turning on them because something they are, something they did, brings back the memory of the past and their failure to be what you expected them to be. Their failure eats at you like an unseen, but wincingly painful, ulcer.

How do you deal with such thoughts? Is there any spiritual balm that can heal the regrets of your past? Yes, there is. And I think, Beloved, it begins with understanding that God is in control. Remember last week you learned from the very Word of God that God has known you before you were formed in your mother's womb. He has always and forever been acquainted with all of your ways. He has promised that the darkness of life will not overwhelm you; it will not permanently bruise you so as to leave you disfigured as a human being for life. God has numbered your days, and the thoughts and plans which He has for you are for your good. God is the Great Redeemer, and that redemption means that He causes all things, no matter what their character, to work together for your good and His glory. The Lord begins our healing process, I believe, with an understanding of His sovereign love and care. With an understanding of the fact that because God is Who He is, because He is our all-knowing, all-powerful Creator and the Sustainer of our life, nothing that has happened to us can thwart His purpose for our life.

All of your past, Beloved, has a purpose in God's sovereign plan. However, Satan would have you believe otherwise. Satan is a liar, a murderer, the destroyer who, since the Garden of Eden, continually whispers in man's thoughts the suggestion that God does not care, that God does not want our good. And so, it is in your mind, your thoughts, that the battle for your healing wages. And it is on this battleground where the victory is won! This then is where we are going to focus our attention—on your thoughts.

Think about what you have just read. Can you relate in any way? How? Write it out.

DAY TWO

As I write this, I want you to know that my life is not free from hurts. There are still wounds which are inflicted by the ones I love, and yet, because I know what I know of the Word of God, I am able to allow God to heal those hurts as they come…one by one, or a whole bunch at one time. But there is also something else I see in these hurts that I experience, and that is the ability to relate to you, to understand where you are coming from, and to be able to tell you that you can live as more than a conqueror through Jesus Christ. If my life were as I dreamed it would be, there would be no hurts, no suffering…and, consequently, I could not be touched with the feeling of your hurts, your infirmities.

Do you know that God refers to believers as a kingdom of priests? Look up the following verses and write them out.

1. Revelation 1:5-6

2. Revelation 5:9-10

Now I want you to go to Hebrews 5:1-3 with me: "For every high priest taken from among men is appointed on behalf of men in things pertaining to God, in order to offer both gifts and sacrifices for sins; he can deal gently with the ignorant and misguided, since he himself also is beset with weakness; and because of it he is obligated to offer sacrifices for sins, as for the people, so also for himself."

These verses may seem a little complicated and hard to understand; however, in their context, these verses in Hebrews are going to point the reader to Jesus as their High Priest appointed by God. The point I want to focus on is the point the author of Hebrews was making about the Levitical priests. The Levitical priests were able to deal gently with those who sinned, because they had sinned also. They were men beset with weaknesses just like those they represented in their priestly duties.

Now although Jesus never sinned, still He was tempted in all points as we are; therefore, He could sympathize with our weaknesses. We have in Jesus a High Priest Who can understand us. And so it is, Beloved, that when you have experienced hurt, you can understand the hurts and rejections others have experienced. And when you have found healing from the balm of Gilead, you can share with them what God has done for you. You become God's "priest" to a hurting world, giving them a message of hope and encouragement! This is what I have seen in my own life; this is what I have seen in Dorie Van Stone's life. *Dorie, The Girl Nobody Loved* is Dorie's story. Because Dorie now lives here and is a part of Precept Ministries, I am constantly aware of how God has redeemed the incredibly horrible wounds of her past and used them to make her a priest unto God. Her story is used mightily to bring hope and encouragement to others.

It is in the light of how God uses our past to minister to others that I want to share the following letter with you. I share it with you well aware of the fact that all honor, glory, and power belong only to our God forever and ever. I share it, though, because I want you to know that, if you will let God redeem a past that you can never change or alter anyway, someday you will find others saying or writing something similar to you...and the joy of being used as His vessel will be worth it all. And I share it with you for another reason, which we will touch on tomorrow.

Here's the letter, and, as you read it, you will see that it is God Who gets the glory. It makes me so rejoice over this woman, for she looks beyond the human instrument to the hand of the One Who uses it:

"I want to thank you for your personal testimony. And to thank God for giving you the grace to be transparent and oh so vulnerable. I hope I can express in words how God used your witness to help me feel a part of the Body of Christ.

"I, too, have an immoral past and will be eternally grateful for the saving blood of Jesus. But I had a problem with my new family (Christians). I felt uncomfortable and unworthy to serve Him. I wasn't sure of just how to fit in, or even if I ever could find my place. Most of the time I felt like the tainted woman trying to be part of the vestal virgins.

"But Jesus released me through you. For I looked at you and saw myself. At last, there was someone just like me. My heart jumped inside of me! I wanted to shout it out! If God could do for you as He has, then He has a place for me also.

"My heart is being cleansed and my mind renewed through what I am learning in the Word through Precept Bible Studies. For the first time in my Christian life, I am being transformed from the inside out. Praise God."

Beloved, if you will believe God and obey Him, He will redeem your past and use it for the glory of His kingdom!

DAY THREE

Yesterday I told you that I had another reason for sharing my friend's letter and that I would tell you that reason today. Did you notice what she said about her heart being cleansed and her mind being renewed through studying the Word of God? Do you know, Beloved, that being in the Word of God is absolutely essential to your healing? That is why I believe there are so many who are not being healed. They have run to drink of the polluted waters of Egypt's Nile, the world's wisdom, instead of turning to the Fountain of Living Waters, Jesus Christ and the Word of God!

Sin disfigures man. Whether sin is committed by us or committed against us, it mars and scars the image of God. Restoration to that beautiful image of Christlikeness comes as we are transformed by the Word of God. I have not only seen it in my life, but have seen, heard, and read of it in the lives of countless others.

Look up Romans 12:1-2 in your Bible, and write out these verses. After you finish writing them, read them aloud three times. Then I suggest you do this three times a day for the rest of the week until you have Romans 12:1-2 memorized. I have found this a very effective way to memorize Scripture.

Now then, Beloved, let me look at these two verses with you. To understand them properly, it is important for you to understand what has gone before in the Book of Romans. The "**therefore**" of Paul's urging his readers to present their bodies as living sacrifices is based on the gospel which Paul has so thoroughly defined and described in Romans Chapters 1-11. God, through Paul, is urging us in the light of all that He has done through the death, burial, and resurrection of His Son to present our bodies to Him as a living and holy sacrifice. Scholars feel that the sacrifice to which God is calling us is like the burnt offering mentioned in the first chapter of Leviticus. A burnt offering was a voluntary offering which was totally given to God and consumed on the altar. No part of the burnt offering was given to the priests—it all belonged to God.

In the light of what God has done to effect your redemption, He is saying to you, in essence, "Will you present yourself to Me to be totally Mine, set apart for Me and for Me alone?"

If God were to say that to you today, Beloved, how would you respond? What would you feel? Say? How would you react? Why? Write out your answer in the integrity born of the fact that God knows your every thought.

DAY FOUR

Some people would be afraid to give themselves without reservation to God. They would be afraid that He might send them to Africa. I don't know why it is always "Africa," but it usually is! Some would be afraid that God might make them be single all of their lives, or never give them husband or wife number two or three if they have been widowed or divorced! Others would be afraid to give themselves totally to God for fear that He might give them cancer or bring their lives to some sort of an abrupt or tragic end! Some are afraid to give themselves to God unconditionally for fear of what He might do to their loved ones. Still others are afraid that God might want to reconcile them to those whom they do not want to love.

Many would be afraid to give themselves to God because God might not allow them to be what they want to be, to do what they want to do, to have what they want to have. They feel that such surrender to God might keep them from the happiness they so desperately crave.

From all that you have learned so far, my friend, in these almost eight full weeks of study, do you think these fears have any weight, merit, or possibility? How would you answer these fears? Write out what you would say to one who presented these fears to you. Be as brief or as lengthy as you feel is necessary. As much as is possible, use the Word of God in your answer.

Were any of these fears yours or akin to yours? Can you accept your answer to your fears?

DAY FIVE

Healing begins with trust. If you do not trust God, then you cannot take Him at His Word. And if you cannot take Him at His Word, then you are refusing the only certain means of healing. You are refusing the healing balm of Gilead. And where else, my friend, will you find a sure cure for your hurts? If the God Who made you and Who knows you, setting His love on you before and behind, above and below, within and without, cannot heal you, how can mere man with his finite wisdom heal you?

O Beloved, if you have not already done so, as much as you know how, will you present yourself to God now, without restraint? If so, write it out. Personalize it by using "I." If not, and if your "why" is any different than it was two days ago, write out why; but do not despair or say there is no hope for you. God is the God of all hope. Continue in your study. Give the Word of God an opportunity to work in your life.

At the beginning of today's study, I said that healing begins with trust. Trust comes from knowing God's Word. And it is in the knowing of God's Word that we are healed and transformed. All of which leads to Romans 12:2 where God tells us: "And do not be conformed to this world, but be transformed by the renewing of your mind, that you may prove what the will of God is, that which is good and acceptable and perfect."

Do you remember that I told you that the battleground where our healing is won is in the mind, in our thought life? We are going to look at that in depth next week, so be patient. We have to learn all of this one principle at a time. Now, look up Matthew 15:18-20, and write it out. (The reason I have you write out the verses at times rather than giving them to you is because it is a good learning device for you. And, Beloved, how I want you to learn these truths! So hangeth, thou, in there!) Oh, yes, as you write out these verses from Matthew 15, let me just remind you that to the Jew, the mind and the heart were the same! So, when you write *heart*, think *mind!*

Now then, can you see why Romans 12:2 is so important? If it is our mind that defiles us or if it is the source of our actions and responses, then it is vital that our minds be renewed so that we will be transformed. Proverbs 4:23 says, "Keep thy heart with all diligence; for out of it are the issues of life" (KJV). And how does one keep his heart or mind? It is done by renewing it through the Word of God. And as the mind is renewed, the man is transformed! This, Beloved, is the cause for such a difference in the maturity level of Christians who have known the Lord for the same amount of time. Or it is the cause of differences in Christians who have experienced the same traumas in their past and yet have experienced greater healing and transformation than others. Levels of maturity or levels of healing are not determined by God. They don't come because God has played favorites! We determine our level of maturity, the depth of our healing, by our response to the Word of God, by our level of faith, our depth of trust, our degree of commitment to obedience.

O Beloved, God has provided everything needed for your healing. It is your responsibility to lay hold of it in faith, to cry out, "Lord, heal my hurts," believing that He will.

As you submit to God, placing your all on the altar, and as you are transformed by the renewing of your mind, then, precious friend, you will know the will of God. And you will find it acceptable, good, and perfect.

DAY SIX

It is a renewed mind that will enable you to deal with your past, for you will be able to handle your past from a different perspective. I want to take you to II Corinthians 5 to show you a marvelous truth which can greatly liberate you from what you might feel are irreparable damages of the past. But before we go there, let me just remind you of a truth which we have already seen. It is Romans 8:28-

30 which assures you that no matter what your past held, no matter how destructive it seemed, your Omnipotent, Omniscient Creator-Sustainer can turn it around and use it for your good. Your loving Father-God will see that it contributes to your becoming more like Jesus.

When your past begins to torment you, when the father of lies comes in torturing you with his whispers of what-might-have-been-if-only, a renewed mind will counterattack with the truth of Romans 8:28-30. It will hold fast in faith to the promise that all will work together for good. We will look at the specifics of how one does this later; may it suffice to say for now that with every act of faith there will come a greater transformation making you more like God and less like the world! This is the victory won by biblical thinking. Note that I said "biblical thinking" not the "power of positive thinking," which in my understanding has its basis in humanism rather than in the Word of God. The power of positive thinking is passed off as "Christian" because it is dressed in Christian terminology; however, a closer look at its tenets will reveal that it is rooted in the flesh! The power of positive thinking stresses "you." **Biblical thinking casts you in faith on what God has done or said.**

Now then, let's look at II Corinthians 5:14-21 which is printed out for you.

1. As you read through the text, mark every reference to **Jesus Christ** with the same distinctive mark (e.g., draw a cross), or mark each in one color. Then in the right hand margin, list everything you learn about Jesus Christ in these verses.

2. Finally mark each reference to **us** in a distinctive way. The **us** will also encompass the following words: **all, they, themselves, we, man**—any reference to the believer. Therefore, mark all of these words in the same way. Then make a list of what you learn from this passage about you as a believer. Put this list at the end of II Corinthians 5:14-21.

II CORINTHIANS 5:14-21

14 For the love of Christ controls us, having concluded

this, that one died for all, therefore all died;

15 and He died for all, that they who live should no

longer live for themselves, but for Him who died

and rose again on their behalf.

16 Therefore from now on we recognize no man

according to the flesh; even though we have known

Christ according to the flesh, yet now we know

Him thus no longer.

17 Therefore if any man is in Christ, he is a new creature; the old things passed away; behold, new things have come.

18 Now all these things are from God, who reconciled us to Himself through Christ, and gave us the ministry of reconciliation,

19 namely, that God was in Christ reconciling the world to Himself, not counting the trespasses against them, and He has committed to us the word of reconciliation.

20 Therefore, we are ambassadors for Christ, as though God were entreating through us; we beg you on behalf of Christ, be reconciled to God.

21 He made Him who knew no sin to be sin on our behalf, that we might become the righteousness of God in Him.

These are quite "renewing" thoughts, aren't they! I can't wait until tomorrow when I can show you how to put these truths into practice! O Beloved, what healing there is for those who will take God at His Word!

DAY SEVEN

As you observed II Corinthians 5:14-21 yesterday, I am sure you saw a number of wonderful absolutes about the child of God. Absolutes are fixed and immutable (unchangeable) qualities, concepts, or standards. One of the absolutes which you should have seen is the fact that Christ died for all, and, therefore, you died.

This is the same truth or absolute which we saw in our study of Romans 6. When Jesus Christ died, God caused us, in His own mysterious way, to die with Him. This means that our **old man**, all that we were through the first Adam before we came to believe in our Lord Jesus Christ, died. In the mind and heart of God, the old you, precious child of God, no longer exists! This is what Paul means when he writes Galatians 2:20. Look it up, and write it out in the space provided.

Now then, what do you see from II Corinthians 5:17 about every child of God? Write out your answer.

As you read that verse, exactly what has passed away?

And what makes you a new creature, besides the fact that old things have passed away? Or to put it another way, what makes us different from people in the world who have not believed in the Lord Jesus Christ so as to be saved? Read Romans 8:9, and write out the verse.

What do you learn from Romans 8:9 that tells you what makes you different from the unbeliever?

Now then, Beloved, I want you to take all of this information and the other truths you have seen this month and fill in the diagram that I have drawn for you.

Put down the following in the appropriate place on the chart:

a. When God chose you for Himself.

b. When you were physically born (the crib symbolizes that).

c. Next to, above, or below the Cross, put the date of your salvation. If you do not know the date, that's fine; put down the approximate time. If you feel that you received Jesus as Savior at an early age but did not have a changed life until a later commitment to Him as Lord, why don't you put down the latter date?

d. Under the line, in the appropriate place, put where the old things were which passed away and where all things became new.

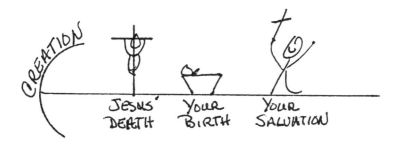

e. Now then, Beloved, put down little x's for your hurts, either because of your own sins or sins committed against you. Put them on the chart in the place where they occurred. When did most of them happen to you? Write out your answer.

If your hurts came before you came to know Jesus Christ, then they belong to a person who died. In II Corinthians 5:16 God says, "Therefore from now on we recognize no man according to the flesh; even though we have known Christ according to the flesh, yet now we know Him thus no longer." What God is saying through Paul in this passage is that once a person dies through identification with Jesus Christ and becomes a new creature, then we don't point to what they were in the past. That is gone! That person, as he or she was, no longer exists!

Stop and meditate on this, Beloved. Are you living shackled to a corpse which is dead? Are you living in the light of your past, or are you living in the light of all that Jesus Christ has accomplished for you at Calvary?

To this question, you may reply, "But I cannot forget what has been said and done to me. I cannot forget my past and all of my failures. It haunts me."

Or you may say to me, "But, Kay, it is what I did after I came to know the Lord Jesus Christ that is tormenting me! How could I ever do that to my Lord?!! I wish it had happened before I knew Him, but it didn't; now what do I do?" You must run to I John 1:9, do what it says, and believe God will do what He says He will do.

Now then, Beloved, let me leave you here to meditate on what you have learned today. Tomorrow and in our next week of study, you are going to learn how to deal moment by moment with the thoughts which torment you. Today I want you to meditate on what you have learned in II Corinthians 5, remembering that your focus is to be on Christ and who you are in Christ, not on what you were before you met Him.

WEEK
9

*Your Mind:
The Battlefield*

For though we walk in the flesh,
we do not war according to the flesh,
for the weapons of our warfare are
not of the flesh, but divinely powerful
for the destruction of fortresses.
II Corinthians 10:3-4

DAY ONE

Those of you who have been wounded and hurt through the verbal, emotional, or physical abuse of others are in a warfare for your very life. Not necessarily for your physical life, unless of course you contemplate suicide or your bitterness is affecting your health, but for your spiritual and emotional well-being which, of course, would then determine your usefulness for the kingdom of God.

Satan will fight long and hard to hold one of his children of wrath (Ephesians 2:1-3) in his dominion of darkness (Acts 26:18), but Satan cannot withstand the saving power of the Spirit of God when the Spirit begins the process of bringing His lost sheep to salvation.

When salvation occurs, according to Hebrews 2:14, Satan's power over a soul is broken because the sin has been completely paid for by the blood of Jesus Christ. However, salvation does not end a person's battle with the forces of the evil one. Satan desires to sift us as wheat, to make us weak and ineffectual servants in the kingdom of God. Having lost us to God, he knows that we are God's forever, yet the reality of that truth does not hinder him from attacking us.

And where does the enemy attack first? If you answered, "In our minds or in our thoughts," you are so right! As we have seen, evil comes from the mind, the heart. As a man thinks within himself, so he is (Proverbs 23:7). That is why in Proverbs we read, "Watch over your heart with all diligence, for from it flow the springs of life" (4:23).

Remember I told you that to the Jew the mind and heart were the same, so when you read *heart,* you can insert *mind.* This is why, Beloved, it is imperative that you have your mind renewed through learning God's Word. It is crucial that you remember and never forget what John 8:44 teaches. Look it up, write it out, and then memorize it. It will help you in the heat of battle!

Satan would tell you that because of what has been done to you, or because of what you have done, you can never be whole, well, healed, set free, or used of God. **THAT IS A LIE!** Anything that takes you back to your past life or "b.c." (before you came to know Jesus Christ as your Lord and Savior), as a means of hurting or tormenting you, is not from God. Mark it down, and don't forget it! God said through Paul, "Henceforth know we no man according to the flesh," or "From now on we recognize no man according to the flesh." God always looks at you as you are in Christ Jesus, and you are to look as He looks.

Satan, however, wants you to focus on what you were. He hates it that you are now a new creature, and, therefore, he wages war on your thought life. If Satan can cause you to focus your thoughts on things which are past, then you cannot dwell or concentrate on what God has before you. This is why Paul wrote, "One thing I do: forgetting what lies behind and reaching forward to what lies ahead, I press on toward the goal for the prize of the upward call of God in Christ Jesus'' (Philippians 3:13-14).

Read through II Corinthians 10:3-7. See what you can observe from this passage on your own. It is a treasure!

These words of Paul's were occasioned because of some slanderous and unkind remarks which were being made about Paul. We will look at that more tomorrow.

II CORINTHIANS 10:3-7

3 For though we walk in the flesh, we do

not war according to the flesh,

4 for the weapons of our warfare are not of

the flesh, but divinely powerful for the destruction

of fortresses (strongholds KJV).

5 We are destroying speculations (imagina-

tions KJV) and every lofty thing raised up against

the knowledge of God, and we are taking every

thought captive to the obedience of Christ,

6 and we are ready to punish all disobedi-

ence, whenever your obedience is complete.

7 You are looking at things as they are out-

wardly. If anyone is confident in himself that he

is Christ's, let him consider this again within him-

self, that just as he is Christ's, so also are we.

1. Now mark every use of the pronoun **we**, and then record everything you learn about **we**.

2. Record what these verses tell us about:

a. our warfare:

b. our weapons:

3. Now then, according to verse 7, what were the Corinthians doing that they should not have been doing? Can you see any parallel to this and what II Corinthians 5:16 is saying? Explain.

4. Begin memorizing II Corinthians 10:3-5. Again I suggest reading it aloud three times each morning, noon, and night until you can say it from memory.

DAY TWO

I do not want us to study this enlightening and liberating piece of Scripture in II Corinthians 10 until I share with you the context in which Paul wrote it. I feel that it will not only encourage you to know that the Apostle Paul understands your hurts, but I also want you to see how God used Paul's hurt as a means of ministering to us, so that we could learn from his experience.

As wonderful as the Apostle Paul seems to us, he did not seem that way to everyone that he met and ministered among. Some whom he had had the privilege of introducing to Jesus Christ did not appreciate Paul and turned against him. Can you imagine the hurt that brings? I have had it happen to me, and, believe me, the pain is real.

If you read what precedes and follows the passage we are studying in II Corinthians 10, it is obvious that some in Corinth were looking down on Paul because of his appearance. I am sure that some of you can relate to that if God did not make you what the world considers normal or beautiful! When I was a child, I was teased because I was so skinny—they called me, "Toothpick," "Broomstick." I didn't have curve one when other girls got theirs, and in those days curves were more in than bones! Now it's bones! I was skinny and called, "Skinny." Those days are now gone forever!

In verse 10 of this chapter, we read, "His letters are weighty and strong, but his personal presence is unimpressive, and his speech contemptible." Our wonderful Apostle Paul (He is my hero.) was unimpressive! Tradition tells us that Paul was short, bow-legged, small. We are also told that he had an eye disease that was repulsive at times because of the yellow, crusty secretion that came forth from his eyes. Can you imagine looking like this in a society that literally worshipped beautiful Greek physiques, erecting gorgeous statues of gorgeous bodies all over the place?!!

Some of the Corinthians were saying that the only thing bold about Paul was his letters. Even his speech left a lot to be desired! Remember again this was a society that loved eloquence and rhetoric. This was a society caught up in worldly wisdom and all that went with it.

The enemy was using the tongues of these people to try to destroy the work God was doing through the Apostle Paul. He was sending out his fiery darts aimed straight at Paul's mind. If he could defeat Paul by getting him to focus his thoughts on all these things and lash back in the same way to the Corinthians, Satan would win a great victory.

But Paul was not ignorant of Satan's tricks, methods, or devices. Paul knew who his enemy was. And that is why Paul reminds the Corinthians that although we walk in the flesh, although we live in a fleshly body, we don't war with fleshly means. And the reason we don't is because our warfare is not with flesh and blood. Paul knew that the weapons of our warfare are not of the flesh, but they are divinely powerful weapons which can destroy strongholds (KJV) or fortresses.

Satan's goal is to set up strongholds or fortresses in our minds. Our responsibility is to stop him. If you know anything about warfare, you know the enemy always tries to set up some sort of a beachhead in his enemy's territory. This gives him an inside base of operations. And as it is in earthly warfare between nations, so it is in spiritual warfare between Satan and his demonic host and God and His angelic host.

When you allow your mind to dwell on things that are not of God or things which are against God, or when you fantasize evil in your mind, you are giving the enemy ground on which he can erect a stronghold or a fortress. This is why Paul says we are "destroying speculations (or imaginations) and every lofty thing raised up against the knowledge of God." If Paul does not destroy the speculations, the imaginations, the thoughts that are contrary to the Word of God, then they can become the means of destroying him.

This is also why Paul goes on to say, "We are taking every thought captive to the obedience of Christ." In other words, whenever a thought comes to Paul's mind, he evaluates it to see if it is pleasing to Christ and in accord with the truth of the Word of God.

Now then, Beloved, I have given you enough to meditate upon for today. But before you go, I want you to take what has been said, think on it in the light of what you observed yesterday, and then write out what you have learned so far that you can personally apply to your life.

DAY THREE

Since possibly many of you will not watch my video teaching tapes on "Lord, Heal My Hurts," I trust that you will indulge me while I draw a little "head" that I use in teaching II Corinthians 10:3-5.

There now, how do you like that? It is quite evident that I am not an artist, and yet I find that many times figures like this, or stick figures, help get the point across and seal a truth in our mind.

If you will notice, I have the devil, Satan, standing outside of the mind, but knocking at the door. Now obviously our minds do not have doors; however, the door with Satan knocking at it is certainly descriptive of what Satan wants—access to our thoughts. He wants to focus our thoughts on things which are contrary to the truth about us as children of God and which are contrary to the teachings of the Word of God. Satan knows that evil proceeds from the heart-mind and that as a man thinks within himself so he is. Therefore, he wants to bring lies or half-truths into our thoughts, so that we might dwell on them. Now, because the enemy is crafty and because he can often disguise himself as an angel of light, he is not going to come knocking at the door of your mind and say, "Hey, hey, hey, Kay baby, this is Satan. Say, how about you and me havin' a little chat there, Kay baby?"

Now that is not Satan's tactical procedure. He is subtle. He never announces who he is unless you are desiring to talk with him! He disguises himself as one of your thoughts. Or he'll drop little suggestions in your mind that, if you don't know where they came from, can really throw you for a loop!

I remember when I was about a year old in the Lord. I had been invited to speak at an evening ladies' meeting at a local church. I had shared my testimony

laced with the Word of God, and God had used it. I was so excited. As I drove my
VW Camper home, I sang song after song to the Lord, making up the words as I
drove along.

Suddenly in the midst of rejoicing in what the Lord had done, this thought
came into my mind, "You did a wonderful job. You are a great speaker." My joy
came to a screeching halt as my mind conversed with itself, "Those were prideful
thoughts! God doesn't use proud people. He resists the proud. Now, I can't speak
anymore because I have pride!"

I was absolutely crushed. I didn't want to be proud. My joy at being used of
God was thrown wounded and bleeding from the chambers of my heart. I stared at
it as a body lying on the street. It had been so beautiful, but now it was dead.

For a while I was shaken. Then light began to dawn. I mused for a few minutes
over the whole incident...those thoughts of pride were not my thoughts...that wasn't
the way I felt about myself. I knew that it was God who had worked, not me. I was
simply His willing and excited and nervous vessel, filled by Him...hmm, where did
those thoughts come from then???

The thinking continued...I have the mind of Christ. That's what I Corinthians
2:16 says, and Christ would not think those kind of thoughts. They are not thoughts
which belong to Him...hmm, and they aren't thoughts I want to think...OH! THEY
ARE FROM THE DEVIL!!!

What release this understanding brought. Joy was resuscitated, jumped up,
brushed herself off, and joined me in another lively chorus of praise! I didn't have
pride; I could be used by my Father!

Can you relate, Beloved? Do you understand what I am saying? Satan made
me think those thoughts were my thoughts! But they weren't, for they don't belong
to the mind of Christ.

What thoughts are you thinking that do not belong to the mind of Jesus? How
can you tell they don't belong to Him? We'll look at that tomorrow, unless of course
you can't wait...and that's all right!

DAY FOUR

Do you ever talk to God in your mind? When you do, do you sometimes feel
that He talks back to you by putting thoughts in your mind?

Whenever I go and speak someplace, I always ask my Father what He wants
me to speak on. A topic, a book of the Bible, or a chapter oftentimes will come to
my mind. However, when it does, I sometimes wonder if they are my thoughts or
God's?

Or I'll ask God to show me whether I should do this or that, and then, when
this or that comes into my mind, I sometimes wonder if it is simply my thought—
me answering me—or if it is God.

How can you and I know whether our thoughts are our own, from Satan, or
from God? How do we check out our thoughts and make sure that they belong to
the mind of Christ? These are critical questions, and the answers will be essential
in dealing with the memories or thoughts of those incidents which have brought
much hurt and pain into your life.

To answer these questions, let me tell you what I do. Then you need to evaluate what I say in the light of the Word of God.

1. The first thing I do with thoughts which come to the door of my mind is to frisk them before I allow them to stay. As I tell my students, "When a thought comes knocking at the door of your mind, you 'Philippians 4:8' it!" You examine each thought to see if it meets the conditions of Philippians 4:8. Look up Philippians 4:8, and write out in list form the conditions that the thought must meet.

IT MUST BE _____

_____

_____

_____

_____

_____

_____

Now then, Beloved, how many of these conditions do you think a thought must meet? Write out your answer and why.

2. When "theological thoughts or doubts" (thoughts or doubts about God, His character, His fairness, His sovereignty, His love, His Word) come to my mind, I bring them beside the teaching of the Word of God. If they do not match God's Word, I reject them immediately; I do not speculate about them. I use God's Word as my plumb line for everything I hear and accept. The symbol—the visual logo—for our ministry is a plumb line. It looks like this:

A plumb line, as I have shared with you before, shows us what is straight. When a carpenter builds, if he is a good carpenter, he never depends upon himself to determine whether something is straight or not. He uses a plumb line; then he knows it's straight!

There are so many who are so perverted or twisted in their doctrine. It is because they have believed Satan's lie that "love and unity" are important, while doctrine is not! They have not examined everything they believe in the light of the whole counsel of the Word of God.

3. When I ask God for direction regarding something I should or shouldn't do, it is never on something that the Word of God speaks to either specifically or in principle. When the Word of God speaks, it stands, and I know what I am to do and what I am not to do. I say this because I have had people say to me, "God told me to_____," and what they are saying is contrary to the Word of God or the character of God. Thoughts which come into your mind which are not in accord with the Word of God are not from God, and, therefore, you must reject them.

4. When I ask God's direction or guidance (e.g., on what I am to teach or which speaking engagements I am to take), then I usually go through the following process. I tell God that I am His and that I only want to do what He wants me to do (Romans 12:1). Then I ask Him to show me what to do. Proverbs 3:5-6 promises me that God will direct my paths. When a subject comes into my mind that I could teach on, I continue to pray and ask God to confirm it by keeping it there or by taking it away. Sometimes a thought will come, and then it will be followed by several other possibilities. I keep asking Him until I have peace in my heart that I have His message.

When it comes to speaking engagements, I automatically know I shouldn't go if Jack says, "No." However, I ask him to prayerfully seek God's will before he gives me an answer. If Jack leaves the choice up to me, I do not always accept the engagement. Again, this is where I must lean heavily on the Spirit's leadership. I mentioned Proverbs 3:5-6 before; therefore, let me write it out for you. "Trust in the LORD with all your heart, and do not lean on your own understanding. In all your ways acknowledge Him, and He will make your paths straight *(direct your paths).*"

Just remember, Beloved, to "Philippians 4:8" your thoughts. It will become a primary means of dealing with thoughts of the past which torment you so.

DAY FIVE

Every thought and every feeling that you and I have must be brought captive to the obedience of Jesus Christ. Our thoughts must submit to the truths of the Word of God or be refused. If you do not learn, Beloved, as II Corinthians 10:5 says, to destroy imaginations and those thoughts which lift themselves above the truth of the Word of God, you will find that those imaginations and thoughts will begin to destroy the joy and peace which are the birthright of every child of God.

One of Satan's tactics is to make you feel rejected by God. His primary target is your relationship with your heavenly Father. He'll give you thoughts such as, "God doesn't love me;" "God has rejected me;" "God can't forgive me for that;" or "I'll never be what God wants me to be, so...." Satan wants you to think God has condemned you and rejected you, and that you, therefore, are separated from Him. Sometimes in order to do this, he will remind you of the rejection you have experienced from others.

The wounds of rejection can hurt greatly. In the light of this, I believe we need to take time to understand rejection and how to deal with it biblically. I want us to look at the rejection which belongs to every child of God, the rejection of man, and then at the one rejection you will NEVER experience—the fact, the absolute truth, that God will never reject you or forsake you. Then when the enemy comes knocking at the door of your mind with all of his "rejection ammunition," you will know how to explode it—in his face, not yours!

You can be certain that rejection, in one form or another, will always come to every child of God. Suffering and persecution are a part of the life of those who belong to Jesus Christ. Remember Jesus suffered rejection from His own, for He came to His own and His own received Him not (John 1:11). "He was despised and forsaken of men, a man of sorrows, and acquainted with grief; and like one from whom men hide their face, He was despised, and we did not esteem Him" (Isaiah 53:3). Don't you think, Beloved, that Jesus can understand and sympathize with your rejection? And remember He was perfect, there was no fault in Him.

So often I have thought, "If only I could have been more perfect, then people wouldn't have rejected me." Sometimes I have groaned and wept over my own inadequacies, my own failures, my own stupidities, and I have thought, "If only I had...," or "If only I hadn't...." I think, "Why didn't I...? I should have.... O why am I...?" Rejection hurts. I know. I understand. All of my mail does not consist of love letters!!!!! Everyone who comes up to talk to me or who calls me is not always pleased with me. Every member of my family does not love me or accept me the way I am. And try as I may, I am not all I should be; I am not perfect! I have to deal with rejection, some of which comes because of my personality and my own inadequacies, and some of which comes because of the gospel.

How do I handle it? By living in the light of all that I am going to share with you. By bringing my thoughts captive to Jesus Christ and listening to God's Word, believing it, and walking in obedience to it. By accepting that "by the grace of God I am what I am" (I Corinthians 15:10) and that I am in the process of being conformed into His image. By remembering Paul's words and making them my own, "Brethren, I do not regard myself as having laid hold of it (Christlikeness) yet; but one thing I do: forgetting what lies behind and reaching forward to what lies ahead, I press on toward the goal for the prize of the upward call of God in Christ Jesus" (Philippians 3:13-14).

How else do I handle rejection? By trying to learn from my mistakes and seeking to turn from that which is not Christlike in character and behavior. By remembering that my Lord, Who was perfect, was rejected. By remembering that even Jesus's half brothers didn't believe on Him and, in essence, rejected Him (John 7:5). By remembering that people whom Paul had led to the Lord didn't like him and talked against him. By remembering the experience of the prophets of old who spoke God's Word and who were rejected by the people and even by priests and kings. By remembering I am God's bondservant and not man's, "For am I now seeking the favor of men, or of God? Or am I striving to please men? If I were still trying to please men, I would not be a bond-servant of Christ" (Galatians 1:10).

I also handle rejection by clinging to the following Scriptures which I want you to look up. As you do, either write them out verbatim, or record the main thought of each. As you do this, personalize them. See how they apply to you. The first two references which you are going to look up explain the rejection which comes with the gospel. There are more verses, but I felt these were all you needed to look up because they show where the rejection can come from.

1. Matthew 10:34-37

2. John 15:18-21

3. Psalm 27:10 (If you have the time, it would be most profitable for you to look at the entire Psalm. It is so rich, and its truths will bless you abundantly. If you do not have time, at least note the setting of verse 10 by reading verses 7-10.)

4. Hebrews 13:5-6 (I would memorize these verses, if I were you! What comfort they have brought me, for I memorized them soon after I was saved.)

Why will God **not** forsake us or leave us? There are two Scriptures which answer this so well. Look them up, and then we will talk about how knowing and remembering these truths will help you handle rejection from others.

The first of these Scriptures is found in Ephesians 1:5-6. Write these verses out in the space that follows. (When you look them up, read Ephesians 1:3-4 also.)

If you looked up verses 5-6 in the New American Standard Bible, then you did not see the word **accepted**, so let me give it to you from the King James Version: "Having predestinated us unto the adoption of children by Jesus Christ to himself, according to the good pleasure of his will, to the praise of the glory of his grace, wherein he hath made us accepted in the beloved." (Years ago, two very dear friends of mine gave me a gold charm with these words engraved upon it, "Accepted In The Beloved," and on the other side they engraved my spiritual birthday, July 16, 1963!)

O Beloved, others may, and will, reject you. God never guarantees that they won't. They may reject you because of your Christianity. They may have rejected you simply because they did not find in you what they wanted. Or maybe you were rejected because you were an inconvenience or burden to them. These are the pains and harvest of a sinful world, but God has overcome sin and all of its pains of death, for He, God Himself, has accepted you in the Beloved. I can say that to you only if you have repented and believed on the Lord Jesus Christ. However, if you haven't, then you need to be saved. Go back to the fourth week of this course and study again the work of Christ upon the Cross and commit yourself to Him; for if you don't, Beloved, you will by your choice be rejected forever by God. Then the rejection of men will seem like nothing!

God wants to engrave you on the palms of His hands through His Covenant of Grace. This truth brings me to another Scripture I want you to look up and write out. You will want to highlight it in your Bible. These are verses that should convince you, without a shadow of a doubt, that God will not and cannot reject you once you are His. They are found in Isaiah 49:14-16:

These are words which God gave to Jerusalem, the city and home of His covenant people—this is who "Zion" is. If Isaiah 49:14-16 is a word to Jerusalem, it is a word to the nation of Israel. If it is a word to them, it is a word to you in the light of the crucifixion and the New Covenant of Grace. There are times, Beloved, when you might think the Lord has forgotten you as His child—times when the pain, the hurt, and the rejection are so bad that you can hardly stand it. But these are times when you need to run into the refuge of your God, into the shelter of His Word, remembering that God cannot forget you, for He has engraved you on the

palms of His hands. Behold the hands of Jesus. Put your finger in the nail pri
and remember that He has loved you with an everlasting love. You are accepted
the Beloved. He will never, never, never leave you or forsake you. God cannot and
will not reject His own. These are the truths you must accept and use to counteract
the lies of the enemy. To be healed of rejection, these truths are what you need to
cling to in faith.

"There is therefore now no condemnation for those who are in Christ Jesus.
Who shall separate us from the love of Christ? Shall tribulation, or distress, or persecution, or famine, or nakedness, or peril, or sword?" Did you think that these
things were signs that God did not love you, that He had forsaken you? Were you
depressed and despairing because you were enduring things such as these? "It is
written, 'For Thy sake we are being put to death all day long; we were considered
as sheep to be slaughtered.' But in all these things we overwhelmingly conquer
through Him who loved us. For I am convinced that neither death, nor life, nor angels, nor principalities, nor things present, nor things to come, nor powers, nor
height, nor depth, nor any other created thing, shall be able to separate us from the
love of God, which is in Christ Jesus our Lord" (Romans 8:1, 35-39).

DAY SIX

Depression is another battle of the mind that hurting people many times have
to fight. While we cannot do an extensive study of depression in this course and
will, therefore, have to leave it for our course on Spiritual Warfare, I want us to
take today to simply familiarize ourselves with this "mind tactic" of the enemy.

Depression is a signal that there is something which is not right; however, that
does not mean that depression is always a symptom of a spiritual problem. Many
men may think so; however, there are many women who know this is not true.
Depression can have a physical cause! It can be a hormonal problem as many
women have discovered when they have almost despaired of ever being free from
depression. I know women who have done everything they could spiritually do and
who have still had to battle depression. Then when their hormonal level was properly taken care of, they were released from depression. Remember, therefore, depression can be physical. When you deal thoroughly with those areas that God has
shown you need to be dealt with in your life in the spiritual and emotional realm,
sincerely seeking God and being willing to be obedient no matter what, and there
is still no relief from depression, ask the Lord for His direction in finding someone
who will check and see if it is a hormonal or biochemical problem. This is not only
true for women, but also for men.

To be depressed is to be "pressed down." If the cause of your depression is not
organic, then it could be that you are depressed because you are dwelling on your
past or because you are angry with God or with man. Or depression can come when
we allow our circumstances to overwhelm us, throwing us into a state of mental
and/or physical inertia. Depression can also be a symptom of unbelief.

We are going to deal with anger and bitterness quite thoroughly later in this study. For now, I want us to look at how we can deal with thoughts of the past which cause constant pain and lead to depression.

The thought I want to give you is a simple one, but one which can bring victory and its joy if you will put it into practice. Let me share a personal illustration which I believe will help. As you know, my past was not a pretty one. It was filled with sin and its awful harvest. After I was saved, I would, at times, find my mind roaming back into my past. What stimulated the thoughts I did not always know. Sometimes they were triggered by some circumstances of life, the seeing of some scene, the hearing of certain music, but often they just popped into my mind. When this happened and I entertained these thoughts, many times I would find depression setting in as I questioned why I had done what I had or as I simply rehearsed the past. Often during these times, I would dwell on my mistakes, my failures, my weaknesses, my sins, my...whatever.

However, as I matured in the Lord, I learned about my thought life and how to apply and live in the light of God's truth, using the same truths that you learned when you studied II Corinthians 5:17. Do you remember the drawing that you filled in, inserting the day of your salvation and when you became a new creature in Christ Jesus? Well, it is applying the truths of II Corinthians 5:17 and Romans 6 to this drawing that can help you deal with your past, so that you don't have to live in depression.

Reason with me from the Word. Everything that you did before you were saved, in essence, is not true of the "new" you! Was your past one of alcoholism, lesbianism, homosexuality, murder, adultery, fornication, abortion, perversion, lying, stealing, cursing, brutality? When you did what you did, you did it under the dominion of the **old man**. I Corinthians 6:9-11 says, "Do not be deceived; neither fornicators, nor idolaters, nor adulterers, nor effeminate, nor homosexuals, nor thieves, nor the covetous, nor drunkards, nor revilers, nor swindlers, shall inherit the kingdom of God. And such **WERE** some of you; but you **were washed**, but you **were sanctified**, but you **were justified** in the name of the Lord Jesus Christ, and in the Spirit of our God."

Before you were saved, were you molested, abused, demeaned, rejected, etc.? When what was done to you was done, it was done to someone who in God's economy has been made new.

As we saw in Romans 6:6, the "old man" died with Christ. II Corinthians 5:14 says, "For the love of Christ controls us, having concluded this, that one died for all, therefore all died." The deeds you did before you came to know Jesus Christ belong to a dead man or woman! Why are you trying then to resurrect them? Why are you mentally chaining your thoughts to a corpse? Dead bodies rot and smell! Have you ever had a dead mouse in your house? I have—several as a matter of fact! When we tried to get rid of the ones which lived in Precept Ministries' old farm house in the winter, the exterminator told us the mice would eat the poison, get thirsty, and head for the creek for water. Some of them must have eaten too much poison! They never got to the water! They never left the house! The stench was overwhelmingly sickening.

O Beloved, the stench of your old man can become overwhelmingly sickening. Just bury the old man; keep the nails on the coffin. If your thoughts take you by the hand to walk into the graveyard of your "b.c." ("before Christ") days, so that you can sit on your old man's tombstone and reminisce or weep for your past, don't go. That is not from God. "Forgetting those things which are behind" is to be your watchword, as it was Paul's (Philippians 3:13). We are to do as II Corinthians 5:16 says, "We recognize no man according to the flesh." You don't look at what you were in the flesh; you look at what you are now in the Spirit, in Christ Jesus: a brand new creature!!!

When your thoughts want to wander over the past, go to God in prayer, saying something like this, "O Father, I am so thankful that that person no longer lives; that that part of me is dead, never to be resurrected or confronted. Thank You that those old things have passed away. Thank You for making me new, brand new. Thank You for forgiving all my sins, for remembering them no more, for putting them behind Your back, for removing them as far as the east is from the west. O Father, forgive me for even beginning to remember, to recall what You have so adequately taken care of, forgiven, and forgotten. Lord, I will bring my thoughts to those things You tell me in Your Word are true of me now."

Now then, Beloved, what from your past is depressing you? Put it away in a prayer of faith. Write out your prayer, then read it aloud.

How earnestly we are praying for you, for your Father God longs that you might believe, listen, obey, and be healed. As I say all of this, I wonder if some of you are hollering at me and saying, "Wait a minute! Don't leave me here! You talked about the things of my 'b.c.' days being buried with my old man, but what if they have been done to my new man? What if they have happened since I came to know Jesus Christ?" Good question. What has happened to the "new man" will be dealt with incident by incident as we look at how to deal with anger, unforgiveness, bitterness, etc.

DAY SEVEN

There are two Psalms in particular which I believe will help you in dealing with thoughts of rejection and other things which can cause depression. They will be especially helpful if you will learn how to pray them back to God.

Using your Bible, read through Psalms 42 and 43 carefully. As you do, mark in a distinctive way or in a distinctive color, the following words: **God** (and all the appropriate pronouns referring to God), **soul, despair, disturbed, rejected,** and **hope**. (If you are hesitant about marking your Bible, don't be. A marked Bible will not only be a continued blessing to you but also to your children and family someday when you are not there and they are missing you dearly.)

When you have finished, Beloved, write out the words which you marked and then list everything you learned from each word.

Our soul is our inner man, the mind, the will, the emotions—what makes you "you," and me "me." In order to help clarify what you observed in marking and listing each use of the word **soul** in Psalms 42 and 43, let me ask you some questions.

1. Why was the psalmist's soul panting and thirsting for God?

2. Have you ever experienced something similar to this? What was the occasion of such a panting and thirsting on your part?

134

3. What is the psalmist dealing with in his relationship to God?

4. Have you ever felt this way about God and your relationship to Him, or His relationship to you? When? Why?

5. Despair is a lack of hope. What do you learn about despair and its cure in these Psalms?

6. Can you see any specific actions from the psalmist's experience which you can follow when you are in despair and feel rejected by God?

As you study these Psalms, if you will pray them back to God, you will find their truths taking root in your heart and bringing forth the fruit of hope.

Let me give you an example of what I mean by praying back Scripture to the Lord. Take the Scripture verse by verse, or thought by thought, and personalize it for yourself or for others. For example, in my quiet time this morning as I read Psalm 9, I felt led to get on my knees and pray back that Psalm to the Lord on behalf of all of my brothers and sisters who are suffering for the gospel of Jesus Christ. As I did, I personalized it for their situation. I also found myself praying for those of you who are taking this course and who are so afflicted by others. The Psalms are especially wonderful to turn into prayer, for they are the out-pourings and musings of the heart. Let me show you what I mean by using the first five verses of Psalm 42, although you could pray through it a verse at a time. Maybe you are hurting over your child, then the prayer might go like this:

"O Father, my heart is panting for You just as the deer pants for the water brook. I am hurting, God, and people are saying that You have deserted me. In my trials, they are asking where You are and why You are allowing me to go through what I am going through. O God, I want to pour out my heart, my soul, to You. Help me in this despair to stop and remember the joy that I have known with You in the past, how I led others with the voice of joy and thanksgiving....

"O Father, I am in despair because I am hurting. You know the pain that I have endured because my child has turned away from You. You know that I feel I have failed in being all that I should have been. But, O Lord, You are greater than all my failures. You can help me in this situation. You can...."

That, Beloved, is how I personalize and pray back Scripture to God. Why don't you try it—at least a verse or two—right now?

As you read and meditate upon these Psalms, it is clear that when one is in despair they need to talk it out with God in prayer. Throughout these Psalms, the psalmist tells God exactly how he feels, but he does not stop there. He remembers and rehearses what God has done, Who He is, and what He will do. The psalmist looks at his past relationship with God. He recognizes that this time of despair too will pass, and he will again praise God. He recognizes that if help is going to come, it is going to come from God! As in the other Psalms, once the heart and needs of the psalmist are laid before God along with the questions and doubts, peace is found in the act of trusting God.

O Beloved, if you are in despair, run to the Psalms. Pray them back to God—aloud—until the sweet relief of faith comes.

WEEK
10

The Battle's On!

Finally, be strong in the Lord,
and in the strength of His might.
Put on the full armor of God....
taking up the shield of faith...
and the sword of the Spirit,
which is the word of God.
Ephesians 6:10,11,16,17

DAY ONE

Wrong thoughts, thoughts which do not meet the qualifications of Philippians 4:8, are to be refused.

I know your question. I can almost hear you screaming, "BUT WHAT DO I DO WHEN THE THOUGHTS WON'T GO AWAY????"

First of all, my friend, you need to remember that you are in a warfare. Satan's strategy is to constantly besiege your mind until he wears down your resistance and then captures your thoughts. Since this is his goal, you can expect a barrage of wrong thoughts constantly hammering away at your defenses. Therefore, don't think that this is strange. It is not strange; it is simply spiritual warfare. You can rejoice, because Jesus is Victor. Victory is assured as long as you let Him be your Captain and do what He says!

You are to resist the devil, and, having done all that you know to do, you are to continue to stand fast. Satan has to flee, because the Word of God says so in James 4:7.

Now then, having said all of that, let's get down to the practical outworking of these truths. I think you will find great help and insight into handling persistent, wearying thoughts by looking at how Jesus dealt with Satan during His temptation. Let's look at the account as recorded for us in the Gospel of Matthew.

As you read this passage, mark every reference to **Jesus** and to the **devil**. Make sure you mark the pronouns also, so that you can tell whether they refer to our Lord or to the devil.

MATTHEW 4:1-11

1 Then Jesus was led up by the Spirit into the wilderness to be tempted by the devil.

2 And after He had fasted forty days and forty nights, He then became hungry.

3 And the tempter came and said to Him, "If You are the Son of God, command that these stones become bread."

4 But He answered and said, "It is written, 'Man shall not live on bread alone, but on every word that proceeds out of the mouth of God.'"

5 Then the devil took Him into the holy city; and he had Him stand on the pinnacle of the temple,

6 and said to Him, "If You are the Son of God throw Yourself down; for it is written, 'He will give His angels charge concerning You'; and 'On their hands they

will bear You up, lest you strike Your foot against a stone.'"

7 Jesus said to him, "On the other hand, it is written, 'You shall not put the LORD your God to the test.'"

8 Again, the devil took Him to a very high mountain, and showed Him all the kingdoms of the world, and their glory;

9 and he said to Him, "All these things will I give You, if You fall down and worship me."

10 Then Jesus said to him, "Begone, Satan! For it is written, 'You shall worship the LORD your God, and serve Him only.'"

11 Then the devil left Him; and behold, angels came and began to minister to Him.

1. List what you learn about Satan's tactics in this passage.

2. In what area(s) did the devil tempt Jesus?

3. Can you see any parallels in the devil's temptation of Jesus and in his temptation of you? Explain your answer.

4. How did the Lord Jesus Christ handle Satan's temptation?

I am sure that by now you have picked up on the fact that Satan persisted in his attempt to seduce Jesus into sin. Once again, the enemy was trying his "wearying, wearing-down attacks," not giving up, not letting up. What a lesson there is for you and me in all of this. We must not give in to the enemy. We are to resist him over and over and over again, rejecting thought after thought that is not pleasing to God or that is not in accord with the Word of God. Everything the enemy says must be brought to the standard of God's plumb line! We are not to allow the enemy to wrest any Scripture from its context to be twisted and perverted for his devilish purpose. We, like Jesus, are to resist the devil, remembering that because of Who is in us we have that authority. Is it not written in I John 4:4 that greater is He Who is in us than he who is in the world?!

When I find myself having to deal with recurring thoughts which are contrary to Philippians 4:8 and which trouble me greatly because they are not from God, then I command the enemy to depart from me in the name of the Lord Jesus Christ. Usually I will say it aloud or, if that is not appropriate, under my breath. I will say something like this, "Satan, those thoughts are not from God. You have no place in me; therefore, in the name of Jesus Christ and by the blood of Jesus Christ, I command you to leave me alone." Revelation 12:11 says, "And they overcame him because of the blood of the Lamb and because of the word of their testimony, and they did not love their life even to death." If Jesus rebuked the devil and told him to leave, and if the devil is overcome by the blood of the Lamb and the word of their testimony, and if I am told to resist him and he will flee (James 4:7), isn't this biblical? Of course!

Now, when you resist the devil, you may find him coming back with a second round of fire, then a third, and a fourth. You must continue to hold your ground in faithful obedience. Victory is yours!

Beloved, let's finish today's study by making a list of the truths you have learned today that you can apply when your adversary the devil goes about as a roaring lion trying to devour your faith (I Peter 5:8). As you make your list, personalize what you have learned. For instance, you might write out your insight like this, "I learned that I must _____"

DAY TWO

If there is any doubt at all in your mind about the reality of the devil and about the warfare a Christian faces once he becomes a child of God, it certainly is removed when one opens the Word of God and allows it to speak for itself! Ephesians 6:10-20 clearly states that we are in a warfare. Read it carefully.

EPHESIANS 6:10-20

10 Finally, be strong in the Lord, and in the strength of His might.

11 Put on the full armor of God, that you may be able to stand firm against the schemes of the devil.

12 For our struggle is not against flesh and blood, but against the rulers, against the powers, against the world forces of this darkness, against the spiritual forces of wickedness in the heavenly places.

13 Therefore, take up the full armor of God, that you may be able to resist in the evil day, and having done everything, to stand firm.

14 Stand firm therefore, having girded your loins with truth, and having put on the breastplate of righteousness,

15 and having shod your feet with the preparation of the gospel of peace;

16 in addition to all, taking up the shield of faith with which you will be able to extinguish all the flaming missiles of the evil one.

17 And take the helmet of salvation, and the sword of the Spirit, which is the word of God.

18 With all prayer and petition pray at all times in the Spirit, and with this in view, be on the alert with all perseverance and petition for all the saints,

19 and pray on my behalf, that utterance may be given to me in the opening of my mouth, to make known with boldness the mystery of the gospel,

20 for which I am an ambassador in chains; that in proclaiming it I may speak boldly, as I ought to speak.

1. In the right hand margin of the text, make a list of what our struggle is against.

2. In the space following or in the right hand margin of the text, list what God tells the child of God to do in this passage. At this point, you need not be specific regarding putting on each piece of the armor; rather, list the commands categorically.

3. List each part of the armor with which the child of God is to be clothed. Next to each piece of armor, write out a brief description of how you believe each piece of the armor relates to you as a child of God.

4. How do you think the armor relates to the Christian's warfare for his or her mind?

5. The devil will do everything he can to keep a child of God from turning to the Great Physician and from applying the healing balm of Gilead to his wounds.

Those who are focusing on their hurts or who are consumed with their pain will have little effectiveness in the kingdom of God. If the devil cannot keep you imprisoned in a cell of unbelief that keeps you from eternal salvation, he will try, at least, to keep the child of God infirmed and ineffective.

In the light of this aspect of Satan's warfare against the saints of the Most High God, can you see any way at all in which an understanding of Ephesians 6 might be used to heal your hurts? For instance, how could the armor of God be effective in the healing process? Be as specific as you can, then hopefully someday you can share these insights with others and be used of God as an instrument in their healing process.

Now, Beloved, pray back to God Ephesians 6:10-20, as I taught you to do with Psalm 42. Personalize these verses in the light of your feelings, your hurts, your needs. As you pray, pray aloud.

DAY THREE

Some hurt because they have a distorted view of God and, consequently, of themselves. They are, as a dear friend wrote, "filled with painful feelings of guilt, self-hatred, fears and worthlessness...caught in a web of performance-oriented acceptance in relationships, including the relationship with Jesus Christ." To look at this friend, whom I will call Karen (not her real name), you would never know that she felt this way. Karen has always seemed to have it together. She is such a godly woman who has ministered to so many through her spiritual gift of exhortation. It is hard to perceive that she was struggling herself to cling to the exhortations of God's Word, which she so sweetly shared with others.

I have known Karen for many years, and yet, sad to say, I never knew until several weeks ago that she was a victim of incest. She shared all of this as she shared what a beautiful work of healing the Lord had performed in her life just recently. As Karen shared this with me, we prayed that God would use her testimony and experience in the Word of God to greatly minister to you.

Under the direction of her pastor, Karen began keeping a journal of Scriptures that she could personalize. Let me quote what she wrote: "This would be Scripture that would affirm who I am in Christ. This I found to be very difficult because I always seemed drawn to that which exposed my shortcomings and failures and that which I felt condemned me." Can you relate, Beloved, or do you know others who can?

As Karen searched the Word, she saw "faulty self-concepts and problem areas" in her thinking. She listed these:

a. Fear and anxiety dominated her life.

b. She felt worthless, inferior, and was extremely self-conscious and disgusted with herself.

c. She felt rejection from peers, family, and friends.

d. She felt guilt and shame intensely for allowing the abuse to occur or for the pleasure which some of it gave her. She had also accepted money from her uncle.

e. Having lost self-respect, she became compliant, accepting wrong from others as something she deserved.

f. Her anger was directed toward herself.

g. She had become performance-oriented in her relationships, especially with God. She sought approval, but she felt she was far short of God's approval.

h. Confidence before God and man was sadly lacking. She always felt inadequate and insecure.

She went on, "As I looked over this list, I became aware that **self and feelings ruled my life**. No wonder I was in such bondage."

God did a mighty work of healing in Karen's life, Beloved, but it did not come by applying the Band-aid of psychology which according to the various philosophies of psychology would point her in one way or another to self—self-love, self-worth, self-acceptance, self-esteem, the power of positive thinking, or positive confession. It was **self** that she was in bondage to. Healing didn't come through turning to any form of psychology. Rather, her healing came by exposure to and obedient faith in the Word of God, the balm of Gilead! It came by being strong in the Lord and in the strength of His might. It came by putting on the whole armor of God.

We will look at more of what my friend shared tomorrow. However, today, let me just give you a word of warning which I believe is greatly needed in Christendom today.

From the very first mention of the devil in Scripture, Satan has sought to separate man from God. His primary tactic is to somehow divert man from the Word of God. If he can do this by getting you to question, doubt, distort, alter, embellish, discredit, or ignore the Word of God, or to substitute "other alternatives" for the Word of God, then he will. He will do anything and everything he can to undermine or dilute or adulterate the Word of God. Remember what God says about His Word—**the Word of God is all you need in order to be perfect, thoroughly adequate for every work of life** (II Timothy 3:16-17). As you studied the armor of God, I am sure you noticed that the Word of God was inherent in every piece of the armor!

The devil's tactic is not only to get man to doubt, ignore, and disobey God's Word, but it is also to get man to doubt God's love, which desires man's highest good. To doubt God's love is to doubt His character. Once the enemy can do this, he cuts you off from the only true and sure source of healing—your Jehovah-rapha, the God Who heals, and the Word of God, the balm of Gilead!

O Beloved, be warned. Know your God. Know His Word. And live accordingly.

DAY FOUR

Karen, who had been the victim of incest as a child, is a faithful student of the Word. But her healing did not come until she began to specifically appropriate and apply the truths of the Word to her particular need.

She wrote, "Gradually the Lord enabled me to find in His Word a truth to counteract the lies I'd been accustomed to hearing. God's view of me was so different from my own and from what I had perceived others to have of me. I would personalize these Scriptures by writing them in a notebook and inserting my name. Then I would read them aloud and savour the truth. I needed to do a study on the character and attributes of God. My concept of God had been faulty, and I longed to grasp His unconditional love and acceptance and to be free of the fear of His wrath.

"I also began studying law and grace from Romans. Because I had been so conditioned to performance, I had not fully laid hold of the blessing of God's grace in my life. I would just weep with joy as this truth unfolded to me! As I began to understand AND accept God's grace, praise became a natural overflow of my heart. I would awaken in the night with a praise song or Scripture on my heart. Most of the mornings I now awaken and begin to praise and thank God that He holds my life in the hollow of His hand. I can trust Him with any circumstance which I might face that day, knowing He will use it to mature me in Christ.

"I did a Bible study on who I am in Christ. Aware of the danger of too much self-preoccupation, my goal was to know God's estimate of His child and to understand His true character. II Corinthians 3:18 took on special meaning as I saw the Word as a mirror. When I looked into the Word, with an unveiled face (totally stripped bare), I could be transformed into His lovely image and reflect Him."

In all of this, Karen was girding her loins with truth, putting on the breastplate of His righteousness. Her feet had been shod with the preparation of the gospel of peace. She was learning where she stood with God and with Jesus Christ, as one who had believed and been saved. The whole process of reading, writing out, personalizing, and savoring the truths of God's Word was enabling Karen to take up the shield of faith with which she would be able to extinguish the fiery darts of the enemy. She was donning her helmet of salvation, renewing her mind, so that she thought and evaluated everything according to the mind of Christ. And in the process of it all, she was honing the sword of the Spirit, the Word of God—the one and only offensive weapon she would ever need to win the conflict of spiritual warfare with the forces of the evil one!

And you, Beloved, through this study are learning to do the same thing. Oh, how I pray that you will not be just a hearer of the Word, but a doer also…so that what you hear will profit you, because it is being united with faith (Hebrews 4:2).

May I suggest that you might want to start your own notebook. As you read through God's Word day by day, you might record those Scriptures which specifically apply to your personal hurts, needs, or misconceptions of God or to your position in Christ. As this ministered so greatly to Karen and to others whom I know, I believe it will do the same for you, especially if you will go over them, read them aloud, and embrace them in faith. Remember to personalize each verse, putting your name in place of each pronoun that refers to a child of God.

Let me give you an example. I might take Colossians 2:9-14: "For in Him all the fulness of Deity dwells in bodily form, and in Him Kay (use your name!) has been made complete, and He is the head over all rule and authority; and in Him Kay was also circumcised with a circumcision made without hands, in the removal of the body of the flesh by the circumcision of Christ; having been buried with Him in baptism, in which Kay was also raised up with Him through faith in the working of God, who raised Him from the dead. And when Kay was dead in her transgressions and the uncircumcision of her flesh, He made Kay alive together with Him, having forgiven her **all** her transgressions, having canceled out the certificate of debt consisting of decrees against Kay and which was hostile to her; and He has taken it out of the way, having nailed it to the cross." Don't forget to savor each truth!

DAY FIVE

We have been looking at the importance of and the power of the Word of God in dealing with the enemy who would keep us from the healing power of Gilead. In the light of this, I think it would be very profitable for you to spend the next two days letting your mind be renewed by meditating on Psalm 119.

As you read through Psalm 119:1-88 in your own Bible:

1. Mark every reference to the Word of God in the same color. The words which refer to the Word of God that you will want to mark are:

      a. **word**   e. **testimonies**

      b. **precepts**   f. **statutes**

      c. **law**   g. **ordinances**

      d. **judgments**

2. Mark each of the following words in a distinctive way: **salvation, hope, revive(d)** and each reference to **God** including the pronoun **Thy**. I usually mark references to deity in yellow.

3. Mark every reference to the word **affliction** and its synonyms.

As you read, personalize those verses which speak to you in a special way by turning them into a prayer to the Lord. For example, when I read verse 38, I might pray, "Heavenly Father, I **do** want you to establish Your Word to me, Your servant. I so desire that Your Word would take root in my heart, renewing my mind and producing a reverence for You, so that I might worship You as You deserve to be worshipped."

The psalmist says, in verse 71, "It is good for me that I was afflicted, that I may learn Thy statutes." You might pray, "Lord, thank You for showing me in these last few weeks through Your Word that You cause all things—my afflictions, my hurts, my pains, even my failures—to work together for my highest good, so that I might be conformed more and more to the image of the Lord Jesus Christ. I praise You, Lord, that I am beginning to see the reality that it truly is good that I was afflicted for through that affliction You have taught me Your statutes." Or maybe you might pray, "Lord, I long for You to bring me to the point that I can say with a full heart towards You that it is good that I was afflicted, that I may learn Your statutes. Thank You for Your faithfulness towards me that will bring me to that point."

"This is my comfort in my affliction, that Thy word has revived me" (Psalm 119:50). It is my prayer for you, Beloved, that you will see that it is the Word of God which God will use to save you out of all your hurts. May God's Word revive you, that you might know His comfort.

DAY SIX

Psalm 119:165 tells us that those who love God's Word have **great peace**, and nothing causes them to stumble! That is God's promise, and His Word is sure!

Read through the remainder of Psalm 119 today, marking it as I suggested yesterday. Give the Lord time to speak to you through these verses as you meditate upon this passage. Personalize thoses verses which have special meaning to you in a prayer to the Lord. You might begin by praying with the psalmist, "Let my cry come before Thee, O LORD; give me understanding according to Thy word" (verse 169).

Isn't it wonderful to see the keeping, sustaining, life-giving power of the Word of God in afflictions?! May you delight in His Word, so that you do not perish in your affliction (Psalm 119:92). Thank Him that His Word is a lamp to your feet, and a light to your path (verse 105). Rejoice that He will sustain you and uphold you according to His Word (verses 116-117)!

When you finish reading Psalm 119, list how this Psalm has ministered to you personally.

DAY SEVEN

As you studied Psalm 119 and noted each use of the word "afflicted," one of the truths that you saw was the fact that affliction causes us to turn to the statutes of God. As you get into the Word and experience its healing balm, you discover God's all-sufficient truths, and what you are learning is never to be kept just for yourself. The comfort which you receive from God in your suffering enables you to minister to others with the same comfort which you received from Him (II Corinthians 1:3-5). This brings me to a very important truth which I want to give you: Having received the Lord Jesus Christ as your Savior, your life has worth, a purpose. God has ordained good works for you to walk in, and all that you have endured in your pain can be used not only for your good but also for His glory if you will make yourself available for ministry.

As Karen wrote out how God had healed her, she said, "My objective in allowing you to use this material is that of ministering to hurting women. Since I am more open about what happened to me, I have 'uncovered' many victims of such abuse.

"In my own Christian walk, there always seemed to have been a missing element of truth in my concept of God (and there was). There was an inner pain that nothing had ever touched—until that day I became aware of the cause. All my life I had had an intense hunger and desire to know God as intimately as possible, but I couldn't seem to break through and enjoy His presence. Kay, thank God the strongholds are now broken down, and His presence is preciously real to me!

"Where would I be today without the background Precept has given me from its beginning, and the personal encouragement you have given me? Thank you for being an affirmer to me!"

I share this last paragraph with you, beloved student, not to boast in an indirect way, for God knows that many times I have failed to be the affirmer, the friend, I should have been. Rather, I share it and this part of Karen's letter because it illustrates a biblical principle which is very vital—that of the ministry in the Body of Christ.

God not only uses His Word in the healing process of His dearly beloved children, but He also uses His children, one with another, to help us through that healing process. God made us members one of another—part of His Body. As you read today, Karen's objective in sharing was to minister to others. How well she knows the vital role the members of the Body of Christ play in a person's healing!

Karen writes that during her six-month healing period, "God has given me precious friends with whom I shared my deepest feelings and greatest fears. They were supportive and encouraging, and when needed they confronted me. They listened with a nonjudgmental heart and helped me see many false concepts that had found root in my thinking. They believed in me as they trusted God to heal my hurts. God used them as an extension of His love for me."

The Apostle Paul was well aware of the crucial role we play in one another's lives. Look up the following Scriptures, and write out what you learn from them in respect to our ministry to one another. Note the various ways we can or are to minister, and why we are to minister.

1. Ephesians 6:18-19

2. Hebrews 10:24-25

3. Galatians 6:1

4. Galatians 6:2

5. I Thessalonians 5:14-15

6. Romans 12:10-11,15

7. Write out Ephesians 4:15-16.

As you fulfill the Scriptures you have studied today and as you exercise your spiritual gifts on behalf of the Body of Christ, you will find that your "proper working" will cause the growth of the Body of Jesus Christ as it is built up in love. Being available to take others by the hand and help them apply and live in the light of God's Word is a much needed ministry in the Body of Christ. Living this way, Beloved, is awesomely rewarding. There is no greater joy that I know of than that of being used of God in the life of another.

All of this brings me to several questions I must lay before you. Is God using you? Are you willing to be open and vulnerable, so that others will find you approachable? Are you usable?

Once you have allowed God to heal you through His Word, you are ready to be used by God in the healing of others. You do not have to be a "professional" counselor to help others. In fact, "professional" counseling, paid counselors, psychologists, and psychiatrists are not God's design—they are man's invention; they are man's substitute for what God intended to happen in the Body of Jesus Christ and what has failed to happen because we have forsaken God's Word and God's call! "The Word of God and the work of the Holy Spirit are sufficient to transform the problems of living and can do so with no help from psychological theories or techniques....For almost two-thousand years the church did without the pseudoscience of psychotherapy and still was able to minister successfully to those burdened by the problems of living."[4]

Jesus Christ was given to us to be our Wonderful Counselor. Look up Isaiah 9:6, and write it out.

In Psalm 119:24, we read, "Thy testimonies also are my delight; they are my counselors" or, to put it literally, "the men of my counsel." Jesus, Wonderful Counselor and the Word of God, studied and applied by the Body of Christ, will give us all the counsel we need for our emotional and spiritual needs. Of course, God may use others to show us His Word, but their effectiveness will be determined by their reliance not on man's words of wisdom, but on God's Word. Their effectiveness will also be determined by their insistence on our dependence upon Jesus, Who is our Wonderful Counselor.

The application then becomes twofold. The first application centers around your healing. Have you buried your hurts and never dealt with them? Or are you willing to acknowledge them and seek God's healing? Do you want to be healed? These are tough questions, but they need to be confronted and dealt with, and that we will do. However, until then, ask God to search your heart so that you can make sure that there is not something with which you haven't dealt. Ask God to show you if there is any hurt you have buried instead of bringing it to the Lord and His Word for healing.

The second application deals with your responsibility to the Body of Jesus Christ. Are you willing to be open and vulnerable so that you can minister to others? Are you willing to make yourself available to be used of God in this way?

1. Look up II Corinthians 1:3-5, and write it out.

2. Now, what do you learn from these verses that pertains to ministering to others? Write it out in your own words.

Finally, Beloved, take a few minutes to talk to your Father. Make yourself available to Him to be used to minister to others—even if it's just in a smile, or a pat, or a short sentence of "I understand" or "I'll pray." Watch what God does!

WEEK
11

How Can I
Forgive?

And forgive us our debts,
as we also have forgiven our debtors.
Matthew 6:12

DAY ONE

"Do you wish to get well?" The question must have been as shocking as a bucket of ice water thrown on his head! It certainly brought him to his senses! There he was face to face with The Truth. There was no more hiding in his infirmity, no more solace in his pain, no more excuses, for what he could have been, could have done, could have had, had he been well. Now he stood looking at the One Who could heal him!

Did he wish to get well? For thirty-eight years, he had been ill. He had spent his days among the infirmed, the sick, the crippled. There were no demands on him—he was afflicted! The world owed him his living, their pity, for seemingly God, or life, had dealt him an evil blow.

Did he wish to get well? It was a valid question.

Of course, he knew how he could be made well. He had it all figured out. That is why he had lain beside the pool of Bethesda under its five porticoes all of these years waiting for an angel to come and stir the waters. For him, the only way to be healed was to get into those stirred-up waters before anyone else. This is why he answered Jesus, "Sir, I have no man to put me into the pool when the water is stirred up, but while I am coming, another steps down before me" (John 5:7).

The man would be healed, but not in the way he had planned. Instead, he merely had to arise, take up his pallet, and walk.

At this point in our study, Beloved, in Jesus's stead, I need to ask you a question, "Do you wish to get well?" Don't let the question offend you. Please don't.

I need to ask that question, for there are some who love their wounds, their hurts, their sickness. Why? There are various reasons. For some, their infirmity brings them the attention and the pity they need. They glory in their afflictions as their hurts are paraded before others. They cause people to take sides. Thus, the ones who have hurt them are despised by others, and the wounded find a twisted comfort in seeing those who wounded them hurt. How would they get even with those who hurt them if they were healed? How could they continue to hurt the one or ones who have hurt them?

Others cling to their hurts and nurse their wounds because their hurts become excuses for what they have become, excuses for their shortcomings and their failures. Their mentality is, "I am what I am because of what I have suffered. You cannot expect anything else!" To be healed would take away their excuse for who they are; it would make them responsible to be what they should be!

Others do not want to be healed because then they could no longer be angry at God! If God healed them, then they would feel an obligation to God—to be what God wants them to be. And that they do not want. They are wrapped up in themselves; they love self. And to relinquish self would be to lose control. Thus, they would rather not be healed.

Others are not sure that they want to be healed, because they wouldn't know how to live if they were healed. There is a fear of change. In a sense, there is a false "comfortableness" in their pain. They have lived and survived this long. Why change?!

Others are so angry, so bitter, so despairing, so demoralized, so numb that it is hard to even think that there is any possibility of ever being healed. To them healing is not even an option—not probable, not possible! No one who desires to be free has to be shackled forever to chains of bitterness and anger. There is hope for the despairing, the demoralized!

Having said all of that, let's get back to the question at hand: "Do you wish to get well?" If your answer is, "Yes," then I must ask you, "Are you willing to get well on God's terms? Will you be made whole? Will you be healed no matter what God says to do? Or do you want to be healed only if you can do it your way and on your terms?"

O Beloved, I am absolutely convinced that there is no wound too great, too extensive, too deep, too damaging that it cannot be healed by the Word of God and the Spirit of God working through His Word. Healing is ours if we will only trust and obey what He says.

In our final weeks of study, we are going to look at some specifics regarding forgiveness, anger, bitterness, love, and acceptance—essentials which must be dealt with if we are going to be healed of our hurts. And in the process of looking at these things, you possibly are going to find yourself face to face with some difficult decisions regarding forgiving others, putting away anger and bitterness, acting in love, and accepting people whom you feel owe you a debt which they have never paid.

As we look at these things, you are going to find the Spirit of God asking you again and again, "Do you wish to get well?" How I pray that your answer will be, "Yes, Lord, heal me, and I shall be healed. Save me, and I shall be saved. I will do whatever You tell me to do. I want to be healed, to be healthy and whole, so that I might serve You fully."

When confronted with this question from the Lord, "Do you wish to get well?" what are your hesitations, your fears, your questions? Write them out, so that you can look back and see how God deals with them to effect your healing.

DAY TWO

Physical wounds that are infected or filled with debris will never heal properly until the wounds are thoroughly cleansed. This is also true in the spiritual and emotional realm of man's inner being. Healing doesn't come by ignoring the infection or the presence of debris or by slapping a bandage over the wound and waiting for it to be healed.

You cannot cover over the infection of hurt or the hot inflammation of the soul's pain and expect to get well. The wound must be discovered, uncovered, debrided, and cleansed thoroughly, if there is to be healing. Please note that I am not saying that you need to uncover things which the Lord has blotted out; rather, I am saying that whatever has been buried or stuffed or denied needs to be exposed, so that the healing balm of Gilead can be applied and, thus, bring healing. [Let me speak a moment about my phrase "blotted out," so that we understand one another. By things which the Lord has blotted out, I mean those things which the Lord has dealt with at the Cross and which are under the blood. I am also referring to those things which you cannot remember or don't remember. I do not believe it is necessary or right—as some would encourage—to go digging around in your past using various unbiblical methods. I call them unbiblical because the Word of God does not use that means, and by now you know I am convinced that the Word is totally adequate—all we need—for healing. If God didn't give us a technique, then we don't need it! In fact, God discourages rummaging around in the attic of your past! In Philippians 3, Paul says, "Forgetting those things which are behind *(past)*." In Isaiah 43:18, God says, "Do not call to mind the former things, or ponder things of the past." If you have buried something and it needs to be dealt with, then God will bring it to your mind as you pray, "Search me, O God…and see if there be any hurtful way *(or way of pain)* in me" (Psalm 139:23-24)].

Healing is a process—a process that comes moment by moment, thought by thought, as you choose to believe God and to walk in diligent obedience to the whole counsel of God's Word in spite of how you feel. Did you notice the word "choose" in that last sentence? Healing comes as you make the choice of believing, obeying, and clinging to the character of God and the Word of God. If you will cling to God as the waistband clings to the waist of a man, then God will make you a person "for renown, for praise, for glory" (Jeremiah 13:1-11).

Now, Beloved, let's begin the healing process by identifying the source of your wound. What is it that you think is causing you to hurt? You might be hurting because of something someone has done to you, or you may be hurting because of something you have done to others or to God. Or you may be hurting because you are disappointed or angry at God because of what you think He has done or has failed to do.

Write out what you think God is showing you as the source of your wound or wounds. Sometimes that is especially difficult to do because we do not want anyone to know about it. We fear that they will be disgusted with us. We fear that they will reject us if they know what we have been involved in. But, Beloved, if God is for you, who can be against you? If God has not rejected you, then what right has man to do so? None, of course, for man is not greater than God! Remember the promise of Jeremiah 29:11. Look it up and write it out before you list your wounds and their sources.

Acknowledging our hurts is essential, and sharing them with others for the purpose of healing is often the means God uses. In fact, I believe this is a vital ministry in the Body of Christ, for God instructs us to bear one another's burdens. In counseling, I have been struck with the wonderful fruit which comes from acting according to James 5:16: "Therefore, confess your sins to one another, and pray for one another, so that you may be healed. The effective prayer of a righteous man can accomplish much."

Time and time again, people have written to me saying, "I have never told this to anyone before in my life, but...." Then in the very writing of their burden, the very sharing of it, there has come a release just by letting another person, whom they can trust, know what they have endured, suffered, or been involved in. I remember a woman who wrote me after I did a television series on incest. The dear woman was in her sixties, married for the third time, and hurting in such a way that it had affected her relationships with her family. She had been sexually molested by her father and her brothers. She was so afraid that if anyone found out about it they would think that she was the cause of it all. For almost 50 years, that precious woman had been suffering needless pain, shame, and guilt...when all the time there was a balm in Gilead, there was a Great Physician Who would have healed her had she only cried out! O Beloved, I know people who have been victims of all sorts of perversion, even bestiality, and they have been healed. Once they had the courage to share, they found another to bear their burdens and, thus, fulfill the Law of Christ (Galatians 6:2). When we bear one another's burdens, we are fulfilling the Law of Christ, for He told us to cast all our burdens on Him, because He cares for us (I Peter 5:7).

I also know many who in their past have gotten involved in lesbianism, homosexuality, or adultery. They are absolutely sickened and nauseated over it, wondering how and why, and now doubting that God could ever use them. I know others who have lived lives of all sorts of perversion, initiating sin rather than being its victim.

If you cannot share how you hurt or how you have been hurt and wounded because of the pain evoked by the very sharing of it, then, Beloved, you can know that it is a very real and infected wound, painful even to the touch. It must be lanced, opened, cleaned out, and treated with the balm of Gilead, so that it can be healed.

What are the wounds, the hurts, the sins, you have ignored or covered over? Write them out so that you can see them and deal with them. I want to be absolutely sure that we do not leave one wound covered and festering. If you do not have enough space here, use another piece of paper. When you finish, write Jeremiah 17:14 after them. If you wrote this on another piece of paper, light a match to it and burn it up. At Calvary, Christ took the baptism of fire for those sins, those wounds, as you will see; therefore, you might as well burn them. What Jesus pays for is gone! (If you want to shout, "Hallelujah," I'll join you!)

In preparation for the coming weeks of study on forgiveness, anger, bitterness, meekness, and dealing with rejection, I want you to see again, Beloved, that everything you have endured, suffered, or experienced can have eternal value if you will view it from God's perspective.

If there is any man in the Word of God who demonstrates this truth, it is Joseph, the son of Jacob (or Israel, as Jacob was later named by God). To see how Joseph demonstrates this precept of life, you are going to have to do some reading in the Book of Genesis. I don't know how much time you have today for this, but I can promise you that the more time you take, the more beneficial it will be. However, because some of you are limited in time by circumstances and "plain old fatigue," let me list what you need to read in Genesis. I'll put an asterisk (*) beside those passages that are imperative if you are going to benefit from today's study. Read one passage at a time.

*Genesis 37:1-36: Note the rejection Joseph suffered from his brothers.

*Genesis 39:1-23: Note the temptation and what Joseph suffered even in his innocence. His suffering and imprisonment lasted for two years, although at the time Joseph had no way of knowing that it would not last a lifetime. Watch his attitude or response, and see what you can learn from it for your own life.

Genesis 40:1-23: Note that although Joseph didn't know it, God was preparing the circumstances which would bring his deliverance. The same is true of you, Beloved, and you can know this because of I Corinthians 10:13: "No temptation (trial or testing) has overtaken you but such as is common to man; and God is faithful, who will not allow you to be tempted (tried or tested) beyond what you are able, but with the temptation (trial or testing) will provide the way of escape also, that you may be able to endure it."

Genesis 41:1-57: Note that when Pharaoh heard Joseph's interpretation of the dream, then Pharaoh's heart was inclined towards Joseph. This put Joseph in the position whereby he would eventually be able to use all that he had suffered for the benefit of his father and family, and even for the benefit of those in Egypt! Beloved,

God does not waste our sorrows. Don't you. Let them be used for the good that God, in His sovereignty, intends.

Because of the famine, Joseph's brothers went to Egypt to buy grain. Through a set of God-ordained circumstances, Joseph helped them by providing grain. He eventually revealed himself to his brothers. Read Chapters 42-44, if you have time.

*Genesis 45:1-5: Note especially verse 5.

*Genesis 50:15-21: Note especially verse 20 and the words "this present result."

When you finish your reading, take the last two passages you had to read and write out how they could be applied to you and your hurts. This, Beloved, ought to give you great hope.

DAY THREE

Beloved, who was it who wounded you? Have you forgiven them?

Or was your wound a self-inflicted wound which came because of your own sin? Have you received God's forgiveness?

There will be no healing, Beloved, apart from receiving and giving God's forgiveness. If you wish to get well, you must do what Jesus says. Nothing less will suffice.

Remember when the disciples came to Jesus in Luke 11, asking Him to teach them how to pray? What did He do? How did He respond? Jesus gave them what we call the Lord's Prayer. The Lord's Prayer was a model prayer, a pattern for prayer, which consisted of seven topical sentences that were reminders of the essential ingredients for effective prayer. This same Lord's Prayer is repeated in Matthew 6:

Pray then, in this way:
"Our Father who art in heaven,
Hallowed be Thy name.
Thy kingdom come.
Thy will be done,
On earth as it is in heaven.
Give us this day our daily bread.

AND FORGIVE US OUR DEBTS, AS WE ALSO HAVE FORGIVEN OUR DEBTORS.
And do not lead us into temptation, but deliver us from evil. For Thine is the kingdom, and the power, and the glory, forever. Amen.'' (Verses 9-13)

With that, Jesus finishes His "model" prayer, but He has more to say regarding forgiveness: "For if you forgive men for their transgressions, your heavenly Father will also forgive you. But if you do not forgive men, then your Father will not forgive your transgression " (6:14-15).

It is difficult to explain, but if we will allow the Word of God to mean what it says without trying to add to it or delete from it, then it is obvious from the words of our Lord that our forgiveness from Him is granted in proportion to our willingness to forgive others. I have known people who have not come to truly know the Lord, so as to be saved and to receive eternal life, because they were unwilling to forgive others. Others have found the salvation they longed for when they were willing to forgive those towards whom they had been unforgiving.

Therefore, Beloved, before we go any further in our study, I want to ask you if there is anyone in your life who has wounded, hurt, or disappointed you in any way, whom you have not forgiven?

Is there anyone whom you refuse to love or to do good to, if you have the opportunity? Ask the Lord to search your heart and to show you anyone whom you have not forgiven. Write their name(s), and then next to it, write out that for which you need to forgive them.

Beloved, if all of this is difficult, if you just cannot bear the thought of completely forgiving someone who has so critically wounded you, write out a prayer to your Heavenly Father, telling Him how you feel and asking Him to help you.

DAY FOUR

One of the clearest explanations of the whole teaching on forgiveness was given to us by our Lord in the form of a parable. The parable was provoked when Peter came to Jesus asking how many times he had to forgive a person who transgressed against him.

Read Jesus's response very carefully. As you read, mark the word **forgive** and all of its synonyms. (By the way, ten thousand talents would have a value of about $10,000,000 in silver content, but it would be worth much more in buying power. A denarius was equivalent to one day's wage.)

MATTHEW 18:21-35

21 Then Peter came and said to Him, "Lord, how often shall my brother sin against me and I forgive him? Up to seven times?"

22 Jesus said to him, "I do not say to you, up to seven times, but up to seventy times seven.

23 "For this reason the kingdom of heaven may be compared to a certain king who wished to settle accounts with his slaves.

24 "And when he had begun to settle them, there was brought to him one who owed him ten thousand talents.

25 "But since he did not have the means to repay, his lord commanded him to be sold, along with his wife and children and all that he had, and repayment to be made.

26 "The slave therefore falling down, prostrated himself before him, saying, 'Have patience with me, and I will repay you everything.'

27 "And the lord of that slave felt compassion and released him and forgave him the debt.

28 "But that slave went out and found one of his fellow slaves who owed him a hundred denarii; and he seized him and began to choke him, saying, 'Pay back what you owe.'

29 "So his fellow slave fell down and began to entreat him, saying, 'Have patience with me and I will repay you.'

30 "He was unwilling however, but went and threw him in prison until he should pay back what was owed.

31 "So when his fellow slaves saw what had happened, they were deeply grieved and came and reported to their lord all that had happened.

32 "Then summoning him, his lord said to him, 'You wicked slave, I forgave you all that debt because you entreated me.

33 'Should you not also have had mercy on your fellow slave, even as I had mercy on you?'

34 "And his lord, moved with anger, handed him over to the torturers until he should repay all that was owed him.

35 "So shall My heavenly Father also do to you, if each of you does not forgive his brother from your heart."

Let me ask you a few questions which, I believe, will help clarify exactly what our Lord is saying in this parable.

1. What does Jesus liken these events to?

2. Whom do you think the king represents in this parable? Why? And whom do you think the king's slave represents?

3. What do you think Jesus is trying to show us in the situation between the two slaves, the one being in debt to the other?

4. Why was the king so upset with the slave whose debt he had forgiven?

5. What was the point of the story—the bottom line? Can you see any parallels between this account and what we studied yesterday from Matthew 6? Explain your answer.

6. What have you learned from this account, and how does it apply to you?

Beloved, think on these things; don't just let them go in one ear and out the other!

DAY FIVE

Before we talk further about forgiving others, it is essential that you realize that, no matter what you have done, God has assured you of complete and absolute forgiveness through the substitutionary death of His only begotten Son. It was through the blood of Jesus Christ that all your sins were paid for—once for all (Hebrews 10:10, I Peter 1:23).

O Beloved, if you do not understand the forgiveness of God, or if you do not appropriate or believe that you have been fully forgiven of all your sins, then, my friend, you will find it very difficult, almost impossible, to forgive those who have deeply hurt you or who have failed to be what they should have been to you as a mate, a mother, a father, a sister, a brother, or a friend.

A guilty conscience before God can wreak havoc and destruction in your relationships with others, in your emotions, and even in your physical body. The cure for a guilty conscience comes in understanding and accepting the grace of God which freely pardons all of your sins through faith in the Lord Jesus Christ. A guilty conscience is shed like filthy rags at the foot of the Throne of God in the Holy of Holies. This is why the author of Hebrews writes, "Since therefore, brethren, we have confidence to enter the holy place by the blood of Jesus, by a new and living way which He inaugurated for us through the veil, that is, His flesh, and since we have a great priest over the house of God, let us draw near with a sincere heart in full assurance of faith, HAVING OUR HEARTS SPRINKLED CLEAN FROM AN EVIL CONSCIENCE and our bodies washed with pure water" (Hebrews 10:19-22). There is no guilt that cannot be cared for at the Throne of God. Your part is to draw near. If you don't, as I said, the guilt will wreak havoc in your life.

There was a pastor who was as straight as an arrow doctrinally, but how he hammered away unrelentingly, unlovingly at his people! His sermons were hard, his walk legalistic, and his expectations demanding. Even his wife flinched in his presence. Nothing was right; there was no pleasing him. He used the word "love," but it seemed all head knowledge. Love's compassionate mercy was never evidenced in his life until he broke and confessed his past to a fellow believer! For years, he had kept his sin bottled up inside, known only to him and a prostitute. Before going into the pastorate, he had served in the army. Based in Korea, he was given two weeks of "R&R" in Japan. It was there in Japan that he had weakened, given in to the temporal cravings of the flesh, and visited a prostitute. He knew God's Word; he knew adultery was a sin; yet, he had yielded!!

Now, after all of his years of serving God—serving in the depth of his dedication, in the strictness of his discipline— he felt he still had not compensated for the guilt that plagued his conscience. Oh, he knew of the Cross, of Christ's death for his sins, but somehow he just couldn't accept God's forgiveness, freely bestowed, freely given for this particular, blatant sin! And because he couldn't accept God's forgiveness, it affected his relationship with his wife, and it affected his ministry as a pastor. How far he was from portraying the Good Shepherd of the sheep, for he was a shepherd who drove his sheep rather than led them. And all because he was driven by the guilt of his sin! He sought to compensate for something that had been covered and dealt with about two thousand years earlier, when Jesus cried, "Tetelestai—paid in full!" All he needed to do was to confess his sin, turn from his sin, and receive by faith the forgiveness that God offered.

Somehow, although he understood the word "grace" to be unmerited favor, he missed, or refused to believe, that it was a covenant of grace, pure grace which Jesus inaugurated on Calvary's tree. Somehow he missed the message of Hebrews 10:15-18: "And the Holy Spirit also bears witness to us; for after saying, 'This is the covenant that I will make with them after those days, says the Lord: I will put My laws upon their heart, and upon their mind I will write them,' He then says, 'And their sins and their lawless deeds I will remember no more.' Now where there is forgiveness of these things, there is no longer any offering for sin."

O Beloved, what will you give to pay for your sins? What can you, in your human impotence, do to pay back the exorbitant debt you owe our righteous and holy God? Work a lifetime? Keep all of His commandments at all times, never faltering once? Always be everything you are supposed to be? Always, totally, unfailingly like Jesus! Can you do that? Of course not! Then what will you do to compensate for the times when you have been less than perfect? What will you do to compensate for the times when you have been willfully, knowingly disobedient to the will of God? Go ahead—try to do your best. Perhaps you try to live a life of righteousness and fail only once. Tell me what you will do with that one and only failure which caused you to miss the mark of His perfection?

Whether your sin has been gross and blatant or delicate and disguised, there is only one way to receive God's forgiveness. It is through the blood of the Lord Jesus Christ—Jesus, the sinless One Who was made sin for you, that you might be made His righteousness (II Corinthians 5:21). God's forgiveness is always an act of grace—that of unmerited, unearned, undeserved, freely-given favor. It is appropriated simply by acknowledging your sin against God and receiving from Him full pardon. It is written in God's infallible Word, "It is a trustworthy statement, deserving full acceptance, that Christ Jesus came into the world to save sinners" (I Timothy 1:15). And He saved us when we were enemies, without hope, ungodly, and helpless (Romans 5:6-10). However, "If we confess our sins, He is faithful and righteous to forgive us our sins and to cleanse us from all unrighteousness" (I John 1:9).

To refuse to believe that you are forgiven forever is to turn your back on the love of God, for God so loved you that He gave His only begotten Son, so that if you believed on Him you would not perish but have everlasting life. God offers you life because Jesus paid for all of your sins, past, present, and future. "But when the kindness of God our Savior and His love for mankind appeared, He saved us, not on the basis of deeds which we have done in righteousness, but according to His mercy, by the washing of regeneration and renewing by the Holy Spirit, whom He poured out upon us richly through Jesus Christ our Savior, that being justified by His grace we might be made heirs according to the hope of eternal life" (Titus 3:4-7).

Beloved, having heard what God says, will you receive His forgiveness? "How?" you ask.

1. First, **agree with God that what you have done is sin, a transgression against God, a rebellion against His will**. Name the sin for what it is. The word "confess" in I John 1:9 is *homologeo* which means "to say the same thing." To confess sin, then, is to acknowledge that what you have done is wrong in God's eyes.

2. **Take the responsibility for that sin**. You cannot blame anyone else. You made a choice to do what you did. "You have not yet resisted to the point of shedding blood in your striving against sin" (Hebrews 12:4). Acknowledge that. Take full responsibility.

3. **Tell God you are willing to make restitution to man if necessary**. This willingness to be right with not only God but also with man, if you have sinned against him, follows the principle laid down for us by our Lord in Matthew 5: 23-24: "If therefore you are presenting your offering (gift) at the altar, and there remember that your brother has something against you, leave your offering there

before the altar, and go your way; first be reconciled to your brother, and then come and present your offering.''

4. Thank God for the blood of Jesus Christ which cleanses you from all sin, and in faith accept His forgiveness. Remember, forgiveness is always on the basis of grace, never merit. Where sin did abound, grace did much more abound (Romans 5:20).

5. Take God at His Word: ''There is therefore now no condemnation for those who are in Christ Jesus'' (Romans 8:1). No matter the feelings, cling in faith to what God says. Don't allow the accuser of the brethren, Satan, to rob you of faith's victory.

6. Thank God for the gift of His Holy Spirit, and tell Him that you want to walk by the Spirit, so that you will not fulfill the lusts of the flesh (Galatians 5:16). A prayer such as this shows genuine repentance.

DAY SIX

Having received forgiveness of sin, how are you to respond towards those who have sinned against you, those who owe you ''a debt'' (so to speak)? Possibly it is your mate, your parent(s), your child, your friend, or your neighbor who has not fulfilled the debt they owe you by virtue of a proper relationship? Or to put it another way, do you need to forgive them because they weren't what they should have been to you? Maybe your wife constantly put you down or withheld herself from you sexually. Maybe your husband abused or neglected you instead of loving you as God commands. Maybe your parents neglected you, demeaned you, abused you, failing you as parents. Maybe your neighbors or friends took advantage of you instead of loving you as they would love themselves. Maybe someone hurt or wounded your loved one.

How are you to respond to them? In order to answer that question, we need to see what God has to say in His Word. Look up the following Scriptures, and record what you learn from them regarding the how's, why's, and wherefore's of forgiveness.

1. Ephesians 4:31-32 (Do you see the connection that bitterness, anger, wrath, clamor, and slander have with unforgiveness? Explain your insights as you look at these verses.)

2. Colossians 3:12-15 (As you look at these verses, do you see any correlation between the character and life style that God is calling us to and the admonition to forgive others?)

3. Finally, how does what you have seen in Colossians and Ephesians relate to what you saw two days ago in your study of Matthew 18:21-35 and Matthew 6:8, 12, 14-15?

The greatest expression of God's love was seen at Calvary's Cross as you heard Jesus say, "Father, forgive them; for they do not know what they are doing" (Luke 23:34). Love forgives.

Think about it, Beloved, and then tomorrow we'll talk about why it is sometimes so hard to forgive. What do you do when you don't think you can forgive?

DAY SEVEN

When a person has suffered so unjustly at the hands of another, it is hard to forgive, especially if the other person isn't repentant or sorry in any way for their sin. Because of the awfulness of their behavior towards us or towards the ones we love, because of the injustice and damage we or our loved ones have incurred because of their sin, many times there is no desire to forgive.

What do you do then? It is crucial and imperative, regardless of how you feel, that you forgive. Remember, if you don't forgive, you will shut yourself off from the forgiveness of God.

But how does one forgive when there is no desire to do so?

1. **You must realize that forgiveness is a matter of the will, not the emotions. To forgive or not to forgive is a matter of choice.** Since God has com-

manded us to forgive others, not to do so is to refuse to obey God. Commands are not options or suggestions the Lord lays before us to be acted upon on the basis of our emotions or desires. Rather, commands are orders issued by our Lord which are to be obeyed regardless of what we feel or think! Take a moment and think on this. Let it sink in.

2. You need to realize that your forgiveness of another does not let that person off the hook with God. Your forgiveness of them doesn't mean that they will not be held accountable to the Lord for what they have done. Let's look at this statement very carefully and point by point if you don't mind.

a. All sin will be judged by God, along with the deeds or works which accompany all of our actions. If a person does not believe on the Lord Jesus Christ so as to be saved, then "there no longer remains a sacrifice for sins, but a certain terrifying expectation of judgment, and the fury of a fire which will consume the adversaries" (Hebrews 10:26-27). "For after all it is only just for God to repay with affliction those who afflict you, and to give relief to you who are afflicted and to us as well when the Lord Jesus shall be revealed from heaven with His mighty angels in flaming fire, dealing out retribution to those who do not know God and to those who do not obey the gospel of our Lord Jesus. And these will pay the penalty of eternal destruction, away from the presence of the Lord and from the glory of His power" (II Thessalonians 1:6-9).

b. Jesus bore mankind's sins in His own body, and yet He forgave those who transgressed against Him when He hung on the Cross. However, if they did not repent and believe on Him, they would still go to hell. Forgiveness was offered, made available, but it is not apart from receiving Jesus Christ as their Lord and Savior. I know that many of you have borne others' sins in your body also, as they have physically, emotionally, sexually, and mentally abused you. Yet, my precious one, you are to forgive them, just as Christ forgave those who transgressed against Him.

c. You are to manifest the character and love of Jesus Christ by forgiving as He forgave you. To refuse to do this is to keep people from seeing the character of Christ. You are the only Bible many people will ever read; therefore, you are to be a living epistle known and read by all men. When you forgive, you are demonstrating the character of God. You are modeling the love of God by forgiving "even as Jesus forgave you."

d. When your forgiveness of them does not lead them to repentance, then they will be held even MORE accountable to God, for they are left without excuse. They have seen with their own eyes and heard with their own ears a demonstration of the reality of the gospel of Jesus Christ. How clearly this principle of "greater accountability" is brought out in Scriptures such as Matthew 11:21-24, 12:41-42, and Revelation 20:11-13.

3. If you are having a hard time, if you are wrestling with forgiving another, you need to ask God to let you take a good, hard, objective look at the Lord's forgiveness of you. Remember, when you forgive someone, it is one sinner forgiving another sinner. Neither of you are, or have been, what you ought to have been. However, in the case of receiving forgiveness from God, it is different. When Jesus Christ forgives us, He is forgiving someone who has sinned against Perfect Holiness!

Take a few minutes to read Luke 7:36-50, and then answer the questions that follow.

LUKE 7:36-50

Now one of the Pharisees was requesting Him to dine with him. And He entered the Pharisee's house, and reclined at the table. And behold, there was a woman in the city who was a sinner; and when she learned that He was reclining at the table in the Pharisee's house, she brought an alabaster vial of perfume, and standing behind Him at His feet, weeping, she began to wet His feet with her tears, and kept wiping them with the hair of her head, and kissing His feet, and anointing them with the perfume.

Now when the Pharisee who had invited Him saw this, he said to himself, "If this man were a prophet He would know who and what sort of person this woman is who is touching Him, that she is a sinner."

And Jesus answered and said to him, "Simon, I have something to say to you." And he replied, "Say it, Teacher."

"A certain moneylender had two debtors: one owed five hundred denarii, and the other fifty. When they were unable to repay, he graciously forgave them both. Which of them therefore will love him more?"

Simon answered and said, "I suppose the one whom he forgave more."

And He said to him, "You have judged correctly." And turning toward the woman, He said to Simon, "Do you see this woman? I entered your house; you gave Me no water for My feet, but she has wet My feet with her tears, and wiped them with her hair. You gave Me no kiss; but she, since the time I came in, has not ceased to kiss My feet. You did not anoint My head with oil, but she anointed My feet with perfume. For this reason I say to you, her sins, which are many, have been forgiven, for she loved much; but he who is forgiven little, loves little."

And He said to her, "Your sins have been forgiven."

And those who were reclining at the table with Him began to say to themselves, "Who is this man who even forgives sins?"

And He said to the woman, "Your faith has saved you; go in peace."

1. How would you describe the Pharisee in this historical account?

2. What do you learn about the woman in this account?

3. What was the point of the story Jesus told to Simon the Pharisee?

4. Contrast the love of the Pharisee and the love of the woman. Weren't they both sinners? What made the difference in their responses to our Lord?

O Beloved, can you see now that the more you comprehend the greatness of God's forgiveness of you, the more you will love? And the more you love, the easier it is to forgive "just as God in Christ also has forgiven you. Therefore be imitators of God, as beloved children; and walk in love, just as Christ also loved you, and gave Himself up for us, an offering and a sacrifice to God as a fragrant aroma" (Ephesians 4:32- 5:2).

Let me share once again what Karen wrote regarding her healing from the incestual abuse inflicted on her by her uncle: "The issue of forgiveness had to be confronted. I visited a dear and trusted friend, also a victim of incest. I had witnessed her peace, contentment and radiant joy in Christ, and I needed to know how she had attained that victory. She related that it had been in a moment of crisis when her marriage was about to fall apart that she knelt and thanked God for giving her the parents He had wanted her to have, and then she expressed gratitude for each person and circumstance of life that God had allowed to touch hers. As she praised and thanked God, she expressed to God forgiveness for what her father had done to her, and she got up from her knees and began to walk in forgiveness and acceptance, and God salvaged her marriage.

"I came home and, in the presence of my pastor, prayed and released my uncle (now deceased) and all others who had offended me from any debt I had felt they owed me. Then I spent another period of prayer alone going through my past, thanking God for being with me through it all, for knowing my downsitting and my uprising, and for being intimately acquainted with all my ways, as Psalm 139:1-6 says. During this prayer God reminded me of many things which He had said of me, His child, in His Word, which I had been rejecting. I recorded each verse as He brought these truths to mind. It was exciting to have God communicating with me in prayer."

Karen forgave. What intimacy it brought with her God, for they were one in heart! O Beloved, will you walk in obedience and forgive, even as Christ Jesus forgave you? To refuse to forgive is to sin. To obey and forgive is to say, "God, I love You, and I am willing to sacrifice self and its desires to prove that." To that, Jesus says, "If anyone loves Me, he will keep My word; and My Father will love him, and We will come to him, and make Our abode with him" (John 14:23). What fellowship, what intimacy, obedience brings!

O precious one, I urge you to take a few moments right now and review what you have learned these past few days about forgiveness. Remember that forgiveness is a matter of your will, a choice to obey God regardless of your emotions. Use these next few moments to ask the Lord to forgive you for your unforgiveness towards those who have wronged you. Will you cry out to your loving, heavenly Father and tell Him that you choose to forgive those persons who have hurt you or who have hurt those whom you love? You might want to write out your prayer to Him.

True forgiveness of another will also bring love. Hatred for that person will be replaced by love. Now as I speak of love, I am not speaking of a sentiment. I am speaking of an action. "Love" is an action verb. As you read through the New Testament, you see love in action. Therefore, if you say you have forgiven a person, but you don't want to have anything to do with them, you need to go back to God and ask Him what is keeping you from loving them. Forgiveness and love are like Siamese twins which cannot be separated, because to do so would bring their death! Stop and think of what love is associated with. Love is part of the ninefold fruit of the Spirit..."love, joy, peace...." As "imitators of God," you are to "walk in love, just as Christ also loved you, and gave Himself up for us, an offering and a sacrifice to God as a fragrant aroma" (Ephesians 5:1-2). Loving one you have forgiven may be hard, but true forgiveness will make such a sacrifice. Jesus didn't just forgive you and refuse to love you! He forgives you and treats you as if you never sinned against Him. That is God's type of forgiveness, and your forgiveness is to be like God's! "If someone says, 'I love God,' and hates his brother, he is a liar; for the one who does not love his brother whom he has seen, cannot love God whom he has not seen. And this commandment we have from Him, that the one who loves God should love his brother also'' (I John 4:20-21).

If you are saying that you cannot love, you may have to deal with anger and bitterness in order to really forgive. We will look at that in the final two weeks. But today won't you say, ''God, out of sheer obedience, I want to forgive. Help me.''? If you will, record it by writing it out.

WEEK
12

But I'm So Angry!

*But let everyone be quick to hear,
slow to speak and slow to anger;
for the anger of man does not achieve
the righteousness of God.*
James 1:19-20

DAY ONE

I had just finished teaching on forgiveness at our Singles Conference, and she came barreling down the center aisle. Dressed in a sloppy, gray sweatshirt and jeans which stretched across a little roll of fat that dropped down below her waist like a small inner tube, it was obvious to me that this woman was not one who enjoyed her femininity. Her hair hung from her head in greasy strands; the darkness of it was in stark contrast to the whiteness of a face that did not have one bit of make-up on it.

I had never seen nor met the woman before, and yet her first words were, ''I can't forgive my father.'' Blurted out in anger through taut lips, it was obvious that I was talking to a woman who was suffering greatly. Why? I did not know. But I intended to find out.

Taking her gently by the arm, I ushered her to the edge of the platform, away from the people, and I seated her so that her back would be to the auditorium.

''Now, darlin', tell me why you cannot forgive your father. What has he done to you?'' I asked, praying at the same time that God would give me great wisdom and that He would love this woman through me.

''My father got me pregnant and then made me have an abortion. Then he got me pregnant again, and this time I had the baby. But my baby was deformed and died. He said that I was a slut, that I had been messing around with boys. But that was a lie. After all that my dad did to me, I didn't want anyone to touch me. Then he got me pregnant again, and this time I moved out.'' The words gushed from her mouth like a dam bursting. There was no stopping the rush of them. ''My baby was born deformed, but she lived for a year. When she died, I didn't want to live, and I tried to kill myself. They put me in a mental hospital and said that I had to have group therapy with my family. When I told them what my father did to me, he jumped up, pointed his finger at me, and yelled that I was lying and that I was a no good slut, just a tramp. My mother jumped up and yelled the same thing at me. So I shut my mouth, and I didn't say a word for months. I cannot forgive my father.''

As suddenly as she began her story, talking almost without breathing, she stopped. She hadn't looked at me the whole time; she had stared only at her feet.

My immediate response to this horrible account was, ''That makes me so angry.''

With that, her head shot up as she said, ''What?''

''What your father did to you. It makes me angry.''

Her big, brown eyes searched mine. Tears began rolling down her cheeks. ''No one has ever said that before,'' she said, as I reached up to wipe them off her chin. Her words were so soft, so incredibly tender.

''Oh, darlin', not only does it make me angry, but it makes God angry, too. Far more angry. God hates what your father did to you.''

These were our first words to each other—words that initiated her healing process. A healing that began when she found out that God, also, was angry at her father's sin. That weekend she chose to forgive her father. Three years have passed since then, and, although I don't have time to tell you all of the wonderful things that have happened, I want you to know that now she loves being a woman. You wouldn't recognize her as the same person. She has lost weight, takes good care of herself, is married, and recently became a mother. No longer is she afraid of her femininity. No longer does she hide it for fear it might be violated. She has learned to lean upon God's Word, to trust Him as a Father she never knew.

How wonderful it was to watch God heal her. I think her healing happened so quickly because she became putty in His sovereign hands of love. It all began when my friend was willing to give her anger and bitterness to God and to forgive her father.

Would you be willing to do the same, Beloved, or are you too consumed by anger to let it go and to let bitterness go, so that you might be willing and able to forgive? Write out your answer to this question. This is a question you need to face quite squarely if you want to be healed.

This week I want us to concentrate on anger. I want us to understand this emotion which is not always wrong, but which, if not handled properly, can wreak havoc in you and in your relationship with God and with others.

DAY TWO

As we begin our study on anger, I think it will be profitable for you to have a good understanding of the word **anger** and how it is translated in the Old and New Testaments.

Some of the insights I want to share with you have been gleaned from Lawrence Richard's enlightening and helpful book, *Expository Dictionary of Bible Words*. If you don't have this book, it is a treasure. It fills a unique place in my library, and I am so thankful for all of the work which has gone into it. I cannot recommend it highly enough. If you are looking for a great gift for anyone who studies the Bible, this is it.

There are a variety of words in the Old Testament which express anger. The most common Old Testament words for anger are the verb *kaas* and the noun *ap*. The noun portrays flaring nostrils and emphasizes the emotional impact of anger. *Kaas* is often used to describe God's anger.

Qasap, the verb, and *qesep*, the noun, are often translated "wrath" and are the strongest terms for anger in the Old Testament. *Qasap* "focuses attention on the relational damage done when one party has said or done something that causes hot anger or deep displeasure." [5] The Old Testament words *hemah* and *haron* mean "burning" and describe anger as "heated emotional passion."

The word *ebrah* means "an overflow" or "fury." This word lays stress on the fierceness of the anger. Used of human anger, it suggests "an arrogant pride expressed as implacable fury." [6]

The Greek word which is translated anger in the New Testament is the word *orge* and is understood in contrast to the word *thumos* which is translated "wrath." When you study Ephesians 4:31, "Let all bitterness and wrath and anger and clamor and slander be put away from you, along with all malice," you see wrath and anger used side by side.

W. E. Vine, in his *Expository Dictionary of New Testament Words*, says, "*Thumos*, wrath (not translated "anger"), is to be distinguished from *orge*, in this respect, that *thumos* indicates a more agitated condition of the feelings, an outburst of wrath from inward indignation, while *orge* suggests a more settled or abiding condition of mind, frequently with a view to taking revenge. *Orge* is less sudden in its rise than *thumos*, but more lasting in its nature. *Thumos* expresses more the inward feeling, *orge* the more active emotion. *Thumos* may issue in revenge, though it does not necessarily include it. It is characteristic that it quickly blazes up and quickly subsides, though that is not necessarily implied in each case." [7]

From all of these uses and meanings of anger in both the Old and New Testaments, it is obvious that anger is an emotion which occurs because of something or some event which takes place. In other words, anger is an inward emotion evoked by an outward action, circumstance, or situation. The action, circumstance, or situation may be something we do or fail to do, or it may be something done apart from us or done to us.

Now in the light of what you have learned today, I want you to do two things.

1. List the things that anger you or your reason for being angry.

2. How do you handle anger? Or to put it another way, what do you do when you get angry?

DAY THREE

Contrary to some people's opinion, anger is not always a sin. As I shared in the incident of my friend and her father, there is a righteous anger. God gets angry. His anger is totally justified and is provoked only by sin. One cannot read the Old Testament or the Book of Revelation without seeing the anger of God, nor the consequences of His wrath. Sin—disobedience—does not leave God passive! His righteousness demands indignation, anger, and wrath at that which goes against His character, at that which violates His commandments and precepts of life. As a matter of fact, if you will recall, one of the attributes of God which we studied was His wrath.

I believe, Beloved, if you and I are going to learn to deal with our anger in a biblical way so that we might be healed, then it will help us if we first understand God's anger.

The words **anger, angered**, and **angry** are used approximately 364 times in the Old and New Testaments. Most of these references are to God's anger. Therefore, let me share with you some of the things which make God angry.

As I list these, I will give you Scripture references which you can look up and write out in the space provided.

GOD IS ANGERED:

1. **By injustice**: Exodus 22:22-24

2. **By idolatry**: Deuteronomy 29:18-21, Jeremiah 25:6

3. **By spiritual adultery**—when we mingle with the world, learn their practices, serve their idols, and sacrifice our children to "demons" through our disobedience: Psalm 106:34-40.

4. **When He is betrayed**: Deuteronomy 4:23-26

5. **When He is not listened to**: Jeremiah 25:6-11 (Remember all that you have learned from Jeremiah about listening to God!)

6. **By disobedience to Him**: Joshua 7:1

7. **When His people complain and murmur against Him or His servants**: Numbers 11:1,33; 12:1-9

8. **By unbelief**: Psalm 78:21-22, Hebrews 3:7-12, John 3:36 (Notice the word **wrath** is used here, which points more to the end result of His righteous anger.)

9. **By the ungodliness and unrighteousness of men who suppress truth in unrighteousness**: Romans 1:18 (Note again the use of the word **wrath**.)

10. **When we refuse to do homage to His Son**: Psalm 2:10-12

Now, Beloved, having seen what angers God, there are several other things I want you to see in regard to God's anger.

God's anger is His response to sin, to unbelief (all unbelief is sin). When we read of God's anger, we need to remember that, although His anger is provoked by man's sin, still He is never controlled by His anger. God's anger is always kept in balance by His holiness—and by all of those attributes which make Him God. Therefore, when God expresses anger, it is always expressed within the realm of His character—never contrary to it. His anger is always in harmony with His grace, His love, His mercy, His compassion, and His longsuffering. It is always expressed with the intent of ultimate good and justice and not of evil. "For His anger is but for a moment, His favor is for a lifetime; weeping may last for the night, but a shout of joy comes in the morning" (Psalm 30:5).

This truth is seen throughout the Word of God. How well it is explained in Exodus 34:6-7, "The LORD, the LORD God, compassionate and gracious, slow to anger, and abounding in lovingkindness and truth; who keeps lovingkindness for thousands, who forgives iniquity, transgression and sin; yet He will by no means leave the guilty unpunished...." You might want to look at the entire passage from Exodus 33 and 34 where God deals with Israel's idolatry at the time of the giving of the Ten Commandments.

Another truth you need to remember about God and anger is that He is slow to anger. This statement is made of Him about nine times in the Old Testament. "But Thou, O Lord, art a God merciful and gracious, slow to anger and abundant in lovingkindness and truth" (Psalm 86:15).

The third truth I want you to see is that our Lord Jesus, God in the flesh, felt anger. Remember the two different times, once at the beginning of His public ministry and the other at the end, when He turned over the tables of the moneychangers in the temple? He was righteously angry, and yet righteously controlled, as He drove out the moneychangers with a whip. We know from the testimony of Scripture that Jesus always handled His anger in a way pleasing to His Father, because He always and only did those things which pleased the Father.

What a lesson there is in these truths for us: justifiable or not, **anger is never to control us**. We are to be controlled by the Spirit of God; therefore, our response must be according to His total character. The moment we are manifesting anything but His heart, we are in trouble.

Now then, Beloved, I have had us look at God's anger for three reasons. Let me state them so that you will know my purpose. First I want you to see that when we talk of anger, all anger is not bad; there is an anger which is justified. Secondly, I want you to see that anger, even if it is justified, is never to control you. When anger takes control of you, then you are in trouble, for the wrath of man does not work the righteousness of God (James 1:19-20). Finally, because anger is an emotion experienced by God as well as by man, you and I can know that God understands the emotion of anger and how it can inflame and burn within. However, we must never forget that God's anger is always justified! Our anger may or may not be justified.

Tomorrow we will begin looking at the anger of man: anger as expressed not only towards man, but towards God. Then in the days to come, we will look at what happens when anger is not dealt with in a biblical way. However, we will not stop there, for we will also see how to deal with our anger biblically, so that healing can come into our lives.

DAY FOUR

Before we look at man's anger toward man, I want us to look at anger towards God. If, Beloved, you are going to know healing, then you must learn what to do with anger towards God if you harbor it in your heart now, or if you would ever be tempted to allow it to enter your heart. **Anger at God is never justified**, as you will see.

I want to list the points one by one so you don't miss a single one.

1. **Anger can come because God doesn't operate or conform to our ways or to our understanding**. How well this is seen in Genesis 4:1-8 when God would not accept Cain's sacrifice, or in John 7:23 when the Jews are angry at Jesus for healing a man on the Sabbath. In the case of those who have been hurt by people or circumstances of life, anger can come because they do not understand why, if God is a God of love, He would allow such things to happen to them or to someone they love. Remember my sharing about the hurting woman who, in great bitterness, said to me, "When God gives me back my baby, then I'll believe in Him"? Her precious baby had died in a fire.

2. **Anger can come because of God's judgment**. In I Chronicles 13:11, David gets mad at God because God kills Uzza for touching the ark of the covenant. In the Book of Revelation, men get mad at God for His judgments upon the earth. Even today, there are many who are suffering because of the consequences of their own sin. Yet, they are angry towards God because He brought judgment upon their sin.

3. **Anger can come because we don't like the words of God's servants**. This is seen in so many places; however, for the sake of time, let me give you just one. King Asa gets mad at Hanani when he rebukes him for not relying on the Lord. In his anger, Asa puts Hanani in prison (II Chronicles 16:7-10). The same thing happened to Jeremiah for delivering God's Word. Again, I mention Jeremiah because we began our course in that wonderful, much-needed book.

There are people who will not be healed, because when they hear the truth regarding God from those who are expounding to them the Word of God, they don't like it. It makes them angry when you tell them that they must put away their bitterness, forgive their transgressors, etc. So they walk away with a parting sentence something like this: "Well, if that's the God of the Bible, then you can just forget it. I don't want anything to do with that kind of a God!!" What is sad is that they are cutting themselves off from Jehovah-rapha and His healing balm.

4. **Anger can come because God doesn't judge others when we want Him to or in the way in which we want Him to judge them. Or anger can come when we don't think God is just**. This is demonstrated so graphically by Jonah in the

fourth chapter of that book. Jonah gets angry with God for sparing Nineveh rather than destroying it. As I write this, I think of those who are angry and bitter towards God for allowing the Holocaust and for not destroying Hitler before he committed all of those horrible atrocities. We will cover this type of anger later when we look at Psalm 37.

Beloved, you need to ask the Holy Spirit to search your heart to see if there is any unresolved anger there which you have harbored against God. Get alone in a quiet place, and give yourself uninterrupted time with Him. If the phone rings, just don't answer it. Turn off the radio, the television, the stereo, and be still. Find a piece of paper and a pen, and write down what God brings to your mind. Then I will share with you what you need to do with what God shows you. If He does not show you anything, then pray for others who are doing this study. Intercede for their total healing.

Beloved, we need to look at how one deals with his anger towards God. Read Isaiah 45:20-24, and then I will give you some insights to ponder.

ISAIAH 45:20-24

20 Gather yourselves and come; draw near together, you fugitives of the nations; they have no knowledge, who carry about their wooden idol, and pray to a god who cannot save.

21 Declare and set forth your case; indeed, let them consult together. Who has announced this from of old? Who has long since declared it? Is it not I, the LORD? And there is no other God besides Me, a righteous God and a Savior; there is none except Me.

22 Turn to Me, and be saved, all the ends of the earth, for I am God, and there is no other.

23 I have sworn by Myself, the word has gone forth from My mouth in righteousness and will not turn back, that to Me every knee will bow, every tongue will swear allegiance.

24 They will say of Me, ''Only in the Lord are righteousness and strength.'' Men will come to Him, and all who were angry at Him shall be put to shame.

If you are angry at God, I would suggest that you:

1. **"Declare and set forth your case."** Use what you wrote out a few minutes ago and talk out your anger with God. Verbalize it. Tell God why you are angry. You might want to write it out below.

2. **Turn to God.** Tell Him you recognize that He is God, and because He is God, He does not have to answer to you. He can do whatever He pleases.

3. **Be put to shame for your prideful rebellion in being angry with Him. Confess your sin.** In being angry at God, you have set yourself as His judge, saying in your heart that God is wrong in His dealings and that He is wrong in His character. You, in your anger at God, have thought as mere man that you knew better than God. You determined what was good and what was evil, rather than allowing God to judge it. That is pride; let it be put to shame. Confess that only in Him is righteousness, that you in and of yourself have no righteousness.

4. **Humble yourself before God. Bow the knee. Submit to Him.**

5. **With your mouth, your tongue, swear allegiance to Him as your God, your Lord, your Master.** And "in the LORD," you "will be justified, and will glory" (Isaiah 45:25). Hallelujah and Amen!

DAY FIVE

Just the other day, I got so angry at my husband that I could hardly stand it. Now, this is not the norm for me. Jack and I get along wonderfully, and I am so thankful for that! However, this was an exception on my part.

I was getting ready to go out when something came up that made me unhappy. Thinking Jack would want to know about it, I began to share with him. We stood talking it through...or, should I say, as I was sharing my heart with him, Jack changed the subject right in the middle of our conversation. Here I was pouring out my heart to him when, right in the middle of the conversation, he asked me if I had recorded a check in the checkbook. He had seen the checkbook lying on my desk while we were standing there talking, so he asked! Now, if you are a man, there may seem to be nothing wrong with such an action, but if you are a woman, I am sure you can understand how I felt!

Anger took over!!! And I sinned! Instead of dealing with the anger, I ran it "full speed" and blew it! I was headed for the grocery store, so I left immediately. Jerking up my keys from my desk, I trounced out of our bedroom, pounded down a book on the bench in our entrance hall, and plummeted out the front door. Now I have to tell you that I haven't done something like this in years—not since just before I wrote our "Marriage Without Regrets" course!

The whole time that I was blowing it, I knew I was wrong. Anger was controlling me, and I was walking in the flesh. And although I didn't think Jack should have picked up the checkbook or should have changed the subject, unfortunately that did not excuse my behavior! I had to come back and ask forgiveness.

Why did I get angry? I think it is a question we always need to stop and ask ourselves when we feel the emotion rising within us. It will help us to evaluate the situation and then handle it in a way that is pleasing to God. Therefore, I want us to look at some incidents from the Word of God where others found themselves in situations where they became angry.

1. **Anger can come when people do not deal fairly with us.** This was the case of David and Nabal. David protected Nabal's flocks, but Nabal would not return the favor by giving David's men a share of his harvest. This infuriated David,

who went out to destroy Nabal. It was Nabal's wife, Abigail, who brought David to his senses when she asked David to forgive her husband: "Let no wrongdoing be found in you as long as you live" (I Samuel 25:28, NIV). David forgave Nabal. David brought his anger under God's control. God dealt with Nabal.

2. **Anger can come when we see others are not treated properly.** This is seen so well in Jonathan's feelings towards his father, King Saul. Jonathan was angry over Saul's treatment of David. "Then Jonathan arose from the table in fierce anger, and did not eat food on the second day of the new moon, for he was grieved over David because his father had dishonored him" (I Samuel 20:34).

Doesn't this kind of anger and hurt come when one lives with an alcoholic who abuses the family? When children suffer through a divorce in the home that destroys the other parent or the home? When one lives with another angry or abusive person? The anger comes, but it must be dealt with, for **to harbor anger is sin.** Unchecked, this anger can cause you to mistreat others.

3. **Anger can come just from seeing the sins of others.** Moses certainly experienced this type of anger several times in his leadership of the children of Israel. Look at Exodus 32:19. Normally Moses brought his anger under control, but when he let his anger rule and struck the rock a second time, after God told him to speak to the rock, that outburst of anger cost Moses the promised land. Even after forty years of wandering in the wilderness, he never entered the land of Canaan, because he had responded to the Israelites in anger instead of obeying God. God said to him, "You have not believed Me, to treat Me as holy in the sight of the sons of Israel, therefore you shall not bring this assembly into the land which I have given them" (Numbers 20:12).

4. **Anger can come because of fear of losing our position or our standing with others.** Jealousy can cause anger. This is seen in Saul's response to the praise given David as the women sang, " 'Saul has slain his thousands, and David his ten thousands.' Then Saul became very angry, for this saying displeased him; and he said, 'They have ascribed to David ten thousands, but to me they have ascribed thousands. Now what more can he have but the kingdom' " (I Samuel 18:7-8)?

Remember the incident I shared from my life at the beginning of this course when Tom slapped me? That whole scene was provoked because Tom was angry over the fact that I had found satisfaction and success in modeling, and he was unhappy in his job. O Beloved, do you see how crucial it is that you deal with your anger, "for the anger of man does not achieve the righteousness of God"? (James 1:20)

5. **Anger can come simply because we feel under pressure, inconvenienced, or interrupted. Or anger may result just because we are irritated by another's personality or behavior.** This is seen in I Samuel 17:28-29 when David visits his brothers while their army is being challenged by Goliath. Watch carefully Eliab's words and David's use of the word "now." "Now Eliab his oldest brother heard when he (David) spoke to the men; and Eliab's anger burned against David and he

said, 'Why have you come down? And with whom have you left those few sheep in the wilderness. I know your insolence and the wickedness of your heart; for you have come down in order to see the battle.' But David said, 'What have I done now? Was it not just a question?' "

6. Anger can come towards those whose expectations we cannot fulfill. Such is the cause of Jacob's anger towards Rachel when she gets upset with him because he does not give her children. "Then Jacob's anger burned against Rachel, and he said, 'Am I in the place of God, who has withheld from you the fruit of the womb?' " (Genesis 30:2).

There are many children and mates, and even parents, who are hurting and angry because they could not fill their parents, mates, or children's expectations, whether the expectations were justified or not. This is the problem with many who are effeminate, homosexuals, and lesbians. They couldn't be the man or the woman their parent wanted, and in their anger and frustration, instead of turning to God, they turned to the same sex for love and acceptance.

7. Anger can come from having our sins exposed by others. Sinners do not like to be found out, and their fury can be great. We have already seen this in Jeremiah's life. This is the reason men stoned the prophets God sent them. This is why Balaam beat his donkey! (Numbers 22:21-35)

8. Anger can come from personal pride. When our pride is hurt in any way, there is the temptation to become angry. This is because pride is of the flesh, and, if you cross the flesh, it is going to get indignant. This is seen in a group of soldiers who are sent home by King Amaziah without ever being allowed to fight in a battle. "Then Amaziah dismissed them, the troops which came to him from Ephraim, to go home; so their anger burned against Judah and they returned home in fierce anger" (II Chronicles 25:10).

I have been to a lot of soccer games, because that is the sport in which our three sons did so well. Sometimes you would see one of the players miss a crucial kick, pass, or goal, and, because of this, he would pound his fist on the ground, get angry, and stomp all over the place. This reaction of anger is a display of personal pride! The flesh is disappointed that it blew it! One of the things we taught our sons was that they were never to display their anger in this way. They were to give their mistakes and failures to the Lord and get on with the game. O Beloved, if you are still seething over the past inadequacies of your flesh, give that to the Lord, and get back in the game.

9. Anger can come from being embarrassed by others. This is what King Ahasuerus experienced when Vashti would not do as he asked. "After these things when the anger of King Ahasuerus had subsided, he remembered Vashti and what she had done and what had been decreed against her" (Esther 2:1). Sometimes women or men who turn against their mates, divorce them, or seek to physically hurt them are reacting to pent up anger which has come because they have been humiliated and/or embarrassed for years by their mate.

10. **Anger can also come against those who condemn others or against those who justify themselves before God or before others.** This was the stimulus which provoked Elihu to anger against Job and against his three "friends" (Job 32:1-4).

11. **Anger can come because of the sins of others.** How vital it is that we give this anger to God and remember it is only the right of God to avenge sin. He alone is just and holy and will avenge according to His character. Now as I say this, I also want to say that if God tells us how to deal with particular sins, then we are to carry out His judgments as He tells us in His Word. Absalom burned with anger until he killed his brother Amnon, because Amnon forced himself on his sister Tamar, robbing her of her virginity (II Samuel 13). Tamar was David's daughter, and when Amnon violated her, although David was angry, he did not allow his anger to control him. However, Absalom was a man who never dealt with his anger, even towards his father, and eventually it resulted in his death.

12. Finally, **the wickedness of man, seemingly unchecked, can cause great anger.** And it is this point that I want us to camp on for the remainder of this day. It will take awhile and some digging, but I believe it can be most beneficial in your healing, Beloved. So hangeth, thou, in there!

Have you ever been angry at the wicked...at their wicked deeds? I have, and if it were not for what I know of God's Word, their seemingly unhindered wickedness would give me an ulcer.

What can you learn from God's Word that will keep you from getting an ulcer over the wickedness of men? That will keep your anger in check? Let's look at the first portion of Psalm 37, for there are some wonderful, practical truths in this Psalm that will help you greatly.

Read through Psalm 37:1-15, and mark the following words in a distinctive way so that you can spot them immediately:

a. **fret**   c. **trust**

b. **anger**   d. **wait, rest**

e. every reference to **God** or the **LORD**, along with their pronouns

f. **evildoers, wrongdoers, wicked** (Mark all of these the same way.)

PSALM 37:1-15

1 Do not fret because of evildoers, be not envious toward wrongdoers.

2 For they will wither quickly like the grass, and fade like the green herb.

3 Trust in the LORD, and do good; dwell in the land and cultivate faithfulness.

4 Delight yourself in the LORD; and He will give you the desires of your heart.

5 Commit your way to the LORD, trust also in Him, and He will do it.

6 And He will bring forth your righteousness as the light, and your judgment as the noonday.

7 Rest in the LORD and wait patiently for Him; do not fret because of him who prospers in his way, because of the man who carries out wicked schemes.

8 Cease from anger, and forsake wrath; do not fret, it leads only to evildoing.

9 For evildoers will be cut off, but those who wait for the LORD, they will inherit the land.

10 Yet a little while and the wicked man will be no more; and you will look carefully for his place, and he will not be there.

11 But the humble will inherit the land, and will delight themselves in abundant prosperity.

12 The wicked plots against the righteous, and gnashes at him with his teeth.

13 The Lord laughs at him; for He sees his day is coming.

14 The wicked have drawn the sword and bent their bow, to cast down the afflicted and the needy, to slay those who are upright in conduct.

15 Their sword will enter their own heart, and their bows will be broken.

Now then, Beloved, take each word that you have marked and make a list of everything you learn from these words. Put your list in the following space.

What are God's exhortations or commands to you in Psalm 37:1-15? List them in the following space.

Although we are going to learn how to deal with anger on another day, I do not want us to miss what we can learn from Psalm 37. Therefore, while this Psalm is fresh on our mind, there are some principles I want us to focus on.

From Psalm 37, you can see that the way to deal with anger is first to refrain from it, to turn away from it. We are not to fret over evildoers. Fretting will only lead to anger and to sin. In the midst of frustration and anger over evildoers, you and I are to delight ourselves in our Lord. When God tells us to delight ourselves in Him, I think He is turning our attention to the one and only true source of satisfaction, and that is Himself. So many of our hurts have come or have been compounded, because our expectations of happiness and fulfillment were placed in others rather than in God. Or we looked to the attainment of things for our happiness rather than to the Lord Himself. He is the One Who gives us the desires of our heart, not man.

O Beloved, have you ever thought that maybe the reason you have hurt so badly is because you sought from man what only God could give you? Maybe that is why you are so angry at your husband or wife, your child, or your mother or father! Your delight has been in the arm of flesh rather than in the Lord Himself…and the flesh will always fail. God won't.

The second way you can deal with anger, according to Psalm 37, is to realize that it is God Who shapes your future, not man. Therefore, peace, rather than frustration and anger, will come as you commit your way unto Him, trust in Him, and wait patiently until He brings it to pass. The will of your Sovereign God will not be thwarted. Therefore, do not allow man to frustrate you or cause you to do evil. Trust in your God, the One Who causes all things to work together for your good. Trust is a great cure for anger.

Finally, Psalm 37 assures us that we do not need to vent our anger on evildoers. God will deal with them, for He sees the day of the wicked coming when "their sword will enter their own heart, and their bows will be broken" (37:13,15). He reminds us to follow our Lord Jesus's example who "while being reviled, He did not revile in return; while suffering, He uttered no threats, but kept entrusting Himself to Him (God the Father) who judges righteously" (I Peter 2:23).

DAY SIX

If not dealt with biblically, anger can be very destructive and dangerous. Newspapers and the evening news confirm this daily as they give reports of killings, murders, riots, and international conflicts. Anger can lead to strife, dissension, conflict, and murder. Anger that is not dealt with may not be detected by others as existing within a soul until it explodes. How often we read of people going on a rampage and killing numerous people for no apparent reason—like the man who, in 1984, walked into a MacDonald's restaurant and gunned down innocent people, or the student who went on a shooting spree in his high school, or the placid, postal clerk who went on a destructive rampage! What is going on? I believe that if you checked carefully, you would see that each was harboring unresolved anger and bitterness. How crucial it is that we learn to deal with anger immediately when it arises in our breast.

How can one know if anger has not been dealt with? To put it another way, how can one know if anger is not released and given to God, but is being held within and stored up? What does anger do when it is not dealt with and released to God? Let me give you a list of insights I have gleaned from the Word. Look up the Scriptures, and make a note of what you learn, so that you can have it as a frame of reference.

1. **Anger seeks revenge**: Genesis 49:6-7, I Samuel 25:28,31

2. **Anger is laid up** (is collected in the heart): Job 36:13

and smolders and burns: Hosea 7:6, Proverbs 30:33

and then...

3. **Anger stirs up strife**: Proverbs 29:22

4. **Anger becomes a flood** (i.e., suddenly gushing out, overwhelming, covering): Proverbs 27:4

5. **Anger bears grudges**: Psalm 55:3

6. **Anger accuses**: I Samuel 17:28

7. **Anger brings sinful actions** (transgressions): Proverbs 29:22

8. **Anger can cut us off from friends**: Proverbs 22:24-25

9. **Anger causes us to despise people** (which many times is manifested in the way that we talk to them or about them) and can lead to murder in the heart or in reality: Matthew 5:22

Unreleased anger will eventually lead to bitterness, and bitterness unchecked, as Hebrews 12:15 tells us, will cause trouble and defile many. Therefore, if you are to be healed, you must deal with anger and bitterness before they destroy you and those with whom you come into contact.

DAY SEVEN

We have finally come to the time when we need to see how to deal with our anger towards man. How do we handle this anger? I want us to begin by taking a good look at Ephesians 4:26.
Write out Ephesians 4:26, and memorize it.

List the two things that we learn about our response to anger from Ephesians 4:26.

1.

2.

Ephesians 4:26 begins with a quote from Psalm 4:4: "Be angry, and yet do not sin...." I have typed out Psalm 4 for you because I want you to see the context of this verse which Paul chose to quote in his letter to the Ephesians. Read the Psalm carefully, and then answer the questions which follow.

PSALM 4

1 Answer me when I call, O God of my righteousness! Thou hast relieved me in my distress; be gracious to me and hear my prayer.

2 O sons of men, how long will my honor become a reproach? How long will you love what is worthless and aim at deception?

3 But know that the LORD has set apart the godly man for Himself; the LORD hears when I call to Him.

4 Tremble, and do not sin; meditate in your heart upon your bed, and be still.

5 Offer the sacrifices of righteousness, and trust in the LORD.

6 Many are saying, "Who will show us any good?" Lift up the light of Thy countenance upon us, O LORD!

7 Thou hast put gladness in my heart, more than when their grain and new wine abound.

8 In peace I will both lie down and sleep, for Thou alone, O LORD, dost make me to dwell in safety.

As you probably noted, the fourth verse of this Psalm reads a little differently than the way Paul quoted it. The margin of my Bible has a footnote next to the word "tremble" which says, "I.e., with anger or fear." Next to the word "and" in verse 4, there is another footnote saying that "and" could be translated "but." Thus, it might read, "Tremble with anger, but do not sin." Apparently, the person is so filled with anger, so inflamed or burning that it causes him to tremble. I can understand that, for there have been times when I have been so angry I was shaking just from inward agitation.

How does one handle this depth of anger? Well, I think the psalmist gives us the solution in his Psalm. Let's look at it.

1. From reading the Psalm, what do you think the psalmist is going through? Is his anger justified or unjustified?

2. What is the psalmist's confidence in the midst of this distress?

3. What does the psalmist say to do in the midst of this shaking anger?

4. What can you learn from this Psalm that you can apply to your life? Be as specific and personal as possible.

Now then, let's go back to Ephesians 4 and look at verses 31 and 32:
"Let all bitterness and wrath and anger and clamor and slander be put away from you, along with all malice. And be kind to one another, tenderhearted, forgiving each other, just as God in Christ also has forgiven you."

1. What do you learn about your response to anger and wrath in these verses?

2. How do you think verse 32 relates, if at all, to verse 31?

3. Read Colossians 3:8-17. How do these verses compare with the ones in Ephesians 4?

Now then, let's also take a look at Galatians 5:19-21, which is typed out for you:
"Now the deeds of the flesh are evident, which are: immorality, impurity, sensuality, idolatry, sorcery, enmities, strife, jealousy, outbursts of anger, disputes, dissensions, factions, envying, drunkenness, carousings, and things like these, of which I forewarn you just as I have forewarned you that those who practice such things shall not inherit the kingdom of God."

1. According to these verses, is anger always bad? Is it always a deed of the flesh? Read the passage carefully before you answer. Then when you do answer, explain why you answer as you do.

2. Have you noticed the end of those who habitually practice these deeds as part of their life style? What is it? What does this tell you about outbursts of anger?

Finally, I want you to look at one more passage of Scripture. I have already mentioned a portion of this passage, yet I feel you need to take a good look at it yourself. It is James 1:19-26, which is typed out for you. Read it carefully, and then answer the following questions:

"This you know, my beloved brethren. But let everyone be quick to hear, slow to speak and slow to anger; for the anger of man does not achieve the righteousness of God. Therefore putting aside all filthiness and all that remains of wickedness, in humility receive the word implanted, which is able to save your souls. But prove yourselves doers of the word, and not merely hearers who delude themselves. For if anyone is a hearer of the word and not a doer, he is like a man who looks at his natural face in a mirror; for once he has looked at himself and gone away, he has immediately forgotten what kind of person he was. But one who looks intently at the perfect law, the law of liberty, and abides by it, not having become a forgetful hearer but an effectual doer, this man shall be blessed in what he does. If anyone thinks himself to be religious, and yet does not bridle his tongue but deceives his own heart, this man's religion is worthless."

1. What is God's command regarding anger?

2. What other things does this passage say we are to do?

3. Do you think any of these other admonitions or exhortations could help us handle our anger? How?

4. Why are you to control your anger?

Now then, Beloved, let me give you a summary list of things from God's Word which you can do when you feel anger.

WHEN YOU FEEL ANGER:

1. **Turn from it. Do not let it control you. Be angry and sin not.** Proverbs 29:8,11 says, "Scorners set a city aflame, but wise men turn away anger. A fool always loses his temper, but a wise man holds it back." Ecclesiastes 7:9 says, "Do not be eager in your heart *(hasty in your spirit)* to be angry, for anger resides in the bosom of fools." Proverbs 16:32 reminds me of my husband, "He who is slow to anger is better than the mighty, and he who rules his spirit, than he who captures a city."

2. **Be willing to overlook others' transgressions against you.** This is meekness, not weakness, as you will see next week. "A man's discretion makes him slow to anger, and it is his glory to overlook a transgression. A man of great anger shall bear the penalty, for if you rescue him, you will only have to do it again" (Proverbs 19:11,19).

3. **When someone says or does something which makes you angry, give them a gentle answer.** "A gentle answer turns away wrath, but a harsh word stirs up anger" (Proverbs 15:1). A harsh word stirs up anger in them, but then it can also stir up anger in you!

4. **Deal with your feelings; don't just stuff them.** "Meditate in your heart upon your bed, and be still. Offer the sacrifices of righteousness, and trust in the LORD" (Psalm 4:4-5). In other words, think through your anger, bring your feelings to the Word of God, and then determine that you are going to sacrifice those emotions and desires for the sake of righteousness. As you read through the Psalms, you will find the psalmist over and over again dealing with his emotions, telling God how he feels, and then remembering truth and acting accordingly. Watch for this, I think it will bless you.

5. **Trust in the Lord.** How well Psalm 37 has taught us this. Remember the story of Joseph in the Old Testament. If anyone could justify anger, it would be Joseph; however, Joseph was never ruled by anger. He knew what you need to always remember, and that is: If anyone ever does anything wrong to you, you can

say with Joseph, ''And as for you, you meant evil against me, but God meant it for good in order to bring about this present result, to preserve many people alive'' (Genesis 50:20). Whatever you go through, if you will handle it as Joseph did, you will find God giving you a ministry that will help preserve others.

6. **"Never take your own revenge**, beloved, but leave room for the wrath of God, for it is written, 'Vengeance is Mine, I will repay,' says the Lord'' (Romans 12:19).

O Beloved, because I don't want you to miss anything that God has for you in this study, I want to ask you to do one more thing. List what God has shown you personally in today's study. What verses have specifically spoken to you in regard to the way you deal with anger?

Look up I Peter 5:6-7, and write these verses out.

Take the next few minutes, dear friend, and pray these verses back to the Lord. Let them be your heart's cry as you humble yourself under the mighty hand of your Father God, Who cares for you so perfectly. Confess your anger to Him, and agree with Him that it is sin. Turn from that anger and forsake it, casting all your anxiety, anger, bitterness, hurt on Him Who loves you so.

Now, look back over your study on anger. Review the truths that you have gleaned. Why don't you write out a prayer of commitment to the Lord.

Well, Beloved, this is our study on anger. I know it has been long, but I believe that it has been thorough!

Now, precious one, rest. Cease from anger. You can, if you will choose to obey as an act of your will, for as God's child you have the Enabler, the Holy Spirit, to help you. Of course if you are not truly born again, if you have not recognized Jesus Christ as your Lord and Savior, then, my friend, there will be no true healing apart from Him. I do pray that you realize this. If what you have been studying in this book is not working, I can assure you that it never will until you take that crucial initial step of salvation by bowing before the Lord in total poverty of Spirit, by letting go of your life in exchange for His.

WEEK
13

The Cure For Bitterness

God is opposed to the proud,
but gives grace to the humble.
James 4:6

DAY ONE

The key to dealing with anger and bitterness is **meekness**. Meekness will open the iron doors that have held you captive in a cell of anger and bitterness. Meekness will grant you a peace and freedom like you have never experienced before. When you studied Psalm 37:1-15, you read in verse 11, "But the humble will inherit the land, and will delight themselves in abundant prosperity." Another word for humble is "meek." How well this verse in Psalm 37 parallels Jesus's words in the Sermon on the Mount, when He says, "Blessed are the meek, for they shall inherit the earth."

I don't believe that there is a person born who does not have within their heart some hope, some dream of a life of fulfillment and enjoyment—a desire to receive all that life might offer. I think a way to describe this "hope" is expressed in the term used repeatedly in Psalm 37—the hope, the desire to "inherit the land." In the Sermon on the Mount, "inherit the land" would be expressed as "inheriting the earth"—the earth, which is the Lord's and the fulness thereof, as the Scripture puts it!

Using your Bible, spend the next few minutes reading through the entirety of Psalm 37. Mark those verses which speak of **inheriting the earth**. As you do, you will come up with a wonderful description of those who are meek. Let's look at those verses, for I am sure, Beloved, that you, too, somewhere, even though it may be buried deep within your heart, have that hope of life—of inheriting what is the Lord's and what He intended for man when He created him and before sin sought to rob him of his inheritance.

In verse 9, we see that it is those who wait for the Lord who inherit the land. One of the characteristics of meekness is **trust**. W.E. Vine describes meekness as "an inwrought grace of the soul; and the exercises of it are first and chiefly towards God. It is that temper of spirit in which we accept His dealings with us as good, and therefore without disputing and resisting." [8] Meekness is used of a submissive and trusting attitude toward God that accepts all of God's ways with us as good and, therefore, does not murmur, dispute, or retaliate. It realizes that what comes to us from man is permitted and used by God for our discipline as His children and, thus, for purifying us. Meekness is a trusting attitude that looks beyond circumstances and beyond man to the sovereign God and, bowing the knee, says, "Lord, what pleases Thee pleases me."

From that description of meekness, it is obvious that meekness is not the natural disposition of sinful man, nor is true meekness possible apart from the Spirit of God. Meekness is an inwrought grace of the soul, and it is only possible when Jesus Christ lives within. It is our Lord Who is meek and lowly in heart or, as the New American Standard Version translates Matthew 11:29, "gentle and humble in heart." (The NASB translates **meek** and **meekness** as "gentle" or "gentleness" in the New Testament, while in the Old Testament it is translated "humble" or "afflicted.")

O precious one, do you see the hope, the healing, that can be yours in the very understanding and acceptance of this inwrought grace of meekness? I want to go on, for I have so much more to share with you; yet, it is almost as if I feel the Spirit of God restraining me. These are not truths to be read quickly and then dismissed.

Understanding meekness—embracing it, walking in it—will root out all of the anger and all of the bitterness you have stored in your heart with every wound of life. **Meekness is the cure for bitterness.**

Stop, reread, and meditate on what you have learned today. And then embrace it in prayer. Remember what you have learned of the character and sovereignty of God. Remember the truths you learned about Romans 8:28-30—how God, because He is God, can cause everything in your life to work together for your good. God can take the worst and use it to make you like Jesus. And that, Beloved, is what life is all about!

Oh, bow the knee in prayer, take the definition of meekness, and personalize it. Tell God you will accept His dealings with you as good, and, therefore, you will quit murmuring regarding your past. You will quit disputing with Him over why these things happened. Exchange your anger and your bitterness for His meekness. Tell Him that you will trust Him to use the horrible and difficult things of your life as His instruments of discipline and purification to make you into the image of His Son.

O precious, precious one, if you will do this, you will inherit all that His grace has provided forever and ever and ever. No one can take it from you!

Meditate on these things.

DAY TWO

Meekness waits, as we saw in Psalm 37:9, and, as a result, it inherits the land. Verse 11 tells us that "the humble (meek) will inherit the land, and will delight themselves in abundant prosperity." Oh, you may have suffered greatly in this life. You may have seemed deprived in the world's eyes, and possibly even in your own eyes, but, Beloved, there is a life that you have not yet seen, not yet tasted, not yet experienced, which is so wonderful "that the sufferings of this present time are not worthy to be compared with the glory that is to be revealed to us" (Romans 8:18). Abundant life awaits. The wicked will perish—vanish (37:20), but you will inherit the land.

In Psalm 37:18, we read, "The Lord knows the days of the blameless; and their inheritance will be forever." You are made blameless in Christ Jesus. You walk a blameless life by being filled with, and controlled by, the Spirit. And part of the fruit of the Spirit is meekness (Galatians 5:23—translated "gentleness" in NASB)!

Remember Matthew 5:5 says, "Blessed are the meek: for they shall inherit the earth."(KJV) And Psalm 37:22 says, "For those blessed by Him will inherit the land; but those cursed by Him will be cut off." When you and I are meek, we are walking righteously, for we are walking as Jesus walked. Psalm 37:29 tells us that the righteous will inherit the land and dwell in it forever.

Meekness is that temper of spirit which trusts, commits, rests, and waits in the Lord. This is what Psalm 37 is all about. And the reward for such a spirit is given to us in Psalm 37:34: "Wait for the LORD, and keep His way, and He will exalt you to inherit the land; when the wicked are cut off, you will see it."

"The posterity of the wicked will be cut off. But the salvation of the righteous is from the LORD; He is their strength in time of trouble. And the LORD helps them, and delivers them; He delivers them from the wicked, and saves them, because they take refuge in Him'' (Psalm 37:38-40).

You need not hold onto your anger. You need not seek to get even with your perpetrators, Beloved. In meekness, let go of it all. Lay it at the feet of your Savior. Take refuge in Him. Draw from His strength. Know the awesome, incredible release and peace of letting all anger and bitterness go. The Lord will help you. Don't worry about revenge; in righteousness He will deal with those who have sinned against you and/or your loved ones. Don't let your anger destroy you. What a victory this would give to the wicked! Put away your anger and your bitterness by clothing yourself in His meekness.

When anger hits, meekness will bring it under control. When you walk in meekness, you turn the other cheek... ''love your enemies, pray for those who persecute you in order that you may be sons of your Father who is in heaven; for He causes His sun to rise on the evil and the good, and sends rain on the righteous and the unrighteous. Therefore you are to be perfect, as your heavenly Father is perfect'' (Matthew 5:39, 44-45, 48). Meekness can behave in this manner because it realizes that the insults and the injuries which man may inflict are only permitted and used by God for the chastening and purifying of His child.

Come to Him, you who are weary and heavy-laden with hurt, anger, and bitterness, and He will give you rest. Take His yoke upon you—become His partner. Make the kingdom of God and its glory your goal, your task. Learn from Jesus, for He is meek and humble in heart. Do this, Beloved, and you will find rest—blessed, sweet rest for your souls. You will find His yoke easy and pleasant, and His load light—light, because you are yoked together with the omnipotent One Who is your Burden-bearer.

DAY THREE

Bitterness comes when one does not see or respond to the difficult circumstances of life from a biblical perspective. It is an angry and resentful state of mind which comes from a wrong response to the difficulties of life. Bitterness can be directed towards God, and often it is. Such bitterness can cause a person to despise the blessings which God bestows upon His children. Bitterness can also be towards man, manifesting its presence as an angry and hostile outlook on life which expresses itself in resentment and attacks on others.

If bitterness is not released and forsaken, it will not only trouble the soil of the heart where it grows, but it will produce a fruit which will trouble the life in which it has taken root. It will also defile others.

The passage which teaches us how to deal with bitterness is Hebrews 12, and this passage well suits our study on the healing of hurts. To really appreciate Hebrews 12, you need to understand the context and occasion of the Epistle to the Hebrews. This epistle was a word of exhortation, written to a group of Jews who were undergoing a great testing of their faith. They had endured a ''great conflict of sufferings, partly by being made a public spectacle through reproaches and tribulations, and partly by becoming sharers with those who were so treated'' (Hebrews 10:32-33). Some had been imprisoned because of their faith. Others had suffered loss of property and possessions simply because they were Christians.

Many had suffered ill-treatment. For some, the temptation to forsake their new found Christianity and return to the old covenant style of worship was very tempting! Christianity was a discipline of life which cost greatly, and some were wondering if it was worth it!

The purpose of Hebrews 12 is to encourage these suffering saints to "lay aside every encumbrance, and the sin which so easily entangles us, and...run with endurance the race that is set before us, fixing our eyes on Jesus"(verses 1-2). After saying all of this and then setting before them the example of Jesus Christ, the author of Hebrews explains the nature of what they are enduring. It is the *paideia* of the Lord—the child training, the discipline, which all true children of God experience.

Let's read Hebrews 12:5-15 as printed out, so that we can learn what discipline and bitterness have to do with each other. As you read, mark each use of the word **discipline**. Mark the words **son** and **children** in the same way, since they are one in the same in this chapter. Also mark the pronouns that relate to us, His children: **you**, **your**, **we**, and **our**. Also mark the words **grace** and **bitterness**, and mark each reference to the **Lord**, along with the relative pronouns.

HEBREWS 12:5-15

5 And you have forgotten the exhortation which is addressed to you as sons,

"My son, do not regard lightly the discipline of the LORD, nor faint when you are reproved by Him;

6 For those whom the LORD loves He disciplines, and He scourges every son whom He receives."

7 It is for discipline that you endure; God deals with you as with sons; for what son is there whom his father does not discipline?

8 But if you are without discipline, of which all have become partakers, then you are illegitimate children and not sons.

9 Furthermore, we had earthly fathers to discipline us, and we respected them; shall we not much rather be subject to the Father of spirits, and live?

10 For they disciplined us for a short time as seemed best to them, but He disciplines us for our good, that we may share His holiness.

11 All discipline for the moment seems not to be joyful, but sorrowful; yet to those who have been trained by it, afterwards it yields the peaceful fruit of

righteousness.

12 Therefore, strengthen the hands that are weak and the knees that are feeble,

13 and make straight paths for your feet, so that the limb which is lame may not be put out of joint, but rather be healed.

14 Pursue peace with all men, and the sanctification without which no one will see the Lord.

15 See to it that no one comes short of the grace of God; that no root of bitterness springing up causes trouble, and by it many be defiled.

Now then, make a list of everything you learned about each word that you marked. When you make a list of what you learned regarding us, His children, make sure you don't miss any instructions or commands which are given to us.

Finally, Beloved, write out a brief statement explaining how all of these truths would relate to the healing of hurts. What in this passage would cure your anger and bitterness and would keep you from being victimized by the events of your life?

This study is so very important, my friend. Do you realize how imperative it is that you embrace these truths and live accordingly? There will not be any true, deep, and lasting healing apart from such obedience of faith.

DAY FOUR

By now, my beloved student, having studied meekness, in all probability you have seen for yourself that one of the primary contingencies upon which your healing rests is **ACCEPTANCE**. When I say "acceptance," I am not saying "acquiescence"! To accept is to believe and to submit. To acquiesce is simply to give in, to resign yourself to something or someone.

What must you accept if you are to be healed by the Lord? Although some of what I want to share today is repetitive of truths which we have already covered, I pray that it won't be redundant, but extremely helpful. Let me list from the Scriptures what I believe is essential—crucial—mandatory for total healing. As I use those descriptive words, you can tell how strongly I feel about what I am saying.

1. **I believe it is essential that a person get to know their God and then to ACCEPT HIS CHARACTER AND SOVEREIGNTY.**

Let's look at why we are to accept His sovereignty. If God is not in charge—totally and completely—then whose hands are we in? If someone pulled something over on God so that He was unaware of what was going to happen to us, then how can He work all things together for our good and our Christlikeness? Surely if man, Satan, accidents, or "fate" can do things to us without God's permission or knowledge, then we are in grave trouble, for it would mean that God is not in charge!

When you consider the sovereignty of God, then you need to know, as I have already discussed weeks ago, what this God is like Who rules over all. As you get to know His character, one of the primary attributes of God, which a hurting person needs to understand, is that God is love. God loves you, my friend, no matter what you are like, no matter what you do. God is love, and it is His love that draws you to Him. He is the initiator.

God says, "I have loved you with an everlasting love; therefore I have drawn you with lovingkindness." Love desires your highest good and is willing to pay the ultimate of sacrifices to attain it. And God gave the ultimate for you in killing His

Son for you, when you were a sinner, His enemy. Hurts are healed by unconditional love. Accept His love; accept His character; accept His sovereignty.

2. **Genuine, lasting healing will never come until, and unless, you ACCEPT THE GRACE OF GOD.** There is a three-fold aspect to the grace of God which affects your healing.

First, there must be the acceptance of the saving grace of God, for it is by grace that you are saved through faith. Grace is a gift of God, never as the result of works. When you truly see your sin, and then see your Savior, and then repent and believe, you become partakers of the Covenant of Grace. God takes away your sins and puts His Spirit within you, and He becomes the One Who enables you to live a righteous life. The Spirit dwelling within is also the seal, the guarantee, that God will keep and complete His covenant by redeeming your body and granting you life eternal in His presence.

To me, to accept the grace of God is to accept the fact that Jesus is God, the One Who will deliver you from your sin as you acknowledge that He is Who He says He is and, therefore, that He has the right to rule your life. Over and over again in our counseling, we have seen that accepting and submitting to the deity, to the Lordship of Jesus Christ, is essential to healing.

The second aspect of grace which you must accept, if you will allow the Lord to heal you completely, is that grace keeps you from bitterness. Since I did not discuss it last week, I want us to look at it for a few minutes. Let's look more closely at Hebrews 12:15-16: "See to it that no one comes short of the grace of God; that no root of bitterness springing up causes trouble, and by it many be defiled; that there be no immoral or godless person like Esau, who sold his own birthright for a single meal."

In the midst of trials, of testing, of temptation, you can rest assured that God's grace is sufficient to allow you to handle anything which comes your way. When our heavenly Father allows us, in His sovereignty, to endure the disciplines or chastenings of our child training, we are not to come short of the grace of God. To come short of the grace of God is to fail to appropriate everything which God has provided for us and which is freely given to us on one condition and on one condition only: the condition of faith.

The author of Hebrews uses Esau as an example of one who failed to appropriate God's grace. In a moment of extreme fleshly hunger, Esau despised his birthright in order to gain the temporary satisfaction of his flesh. God's grace was sufficient to help Esau handle his cravings, but Esau did not appropriate it.

O Beloved, do you see the parallel? God's grace is sufficient for any trial, any hurt, any failure. It is yours, unconditionally, for the mere believing. The question is: "Will you appropriate it in faith?" Whatever your hurt, your wound, your past, His grace is sufficient. **ACCEPT HIS GRACE.**

The third aspect of His grace which you need to accept for your healing is in respect to who and what you are. Paul said in I Corinthians 15:10, "But by the grace of God I am what I am." Everything from the time of your conception to right now has gone into that which has made you His and, thus, His co-laborer for the furtherance of His kingdom. This truth may be hard for you to comprehend, but this is what God's Word says, and God does not lie. Remember John 15:16, "You did not choose Me, but I chose you, and appointed you, that you should go and bear fruit, and that your fruit should remain, that whatever you ask of the Father in My name, He may give to you.'' You, Beloved, are God's ''workmanship, created in Christ Jesus unto good works, which God hath before ordained'' for you to walk in (Ephesians 2:10, KJV).

For you to fail to accept these truths and to fail to live in faithful obedience to them is to come short of the grace of God. Paul never allowed the sinfulness of his past, his incarceration, and the subsequent death of Christians, the timing of his salvation, the physical aspects of his unattractive appearance and speech, or his less-than-perfect performance as a Christian to keep him from going forward to a fruitful life for Christ. Because Paul accepted the grace of God in all of its fulness, he was able to say, ''His grace toward me did not prove vain; but I labored even more than all of them, yet not I, but the grace of God with me'' (I Corinthians 15:10).

For God's grace to prove vain in your life is to say, ''I know what God is saying, BUT _____.'' Whatever you would add here would contradict the veracity of His Word and the sufficiency of His grace, for His grace takes your weakness and transforms it into His strength! O Beloved, do you realize that God does not need anything you have; He wants only who you are, so that He can fill you with Himself?

As you move out in faith, accepting His grace, you will find your life having great significance in His kingdom. Many times the significance of your life may remain unseen to you, but it is not unseen to God. It is all a matter of faith, of belief. Grace will do the rest! Now then, do not let His grace be in vain; accept it!

3. **The third thing you need to accept in order to experience full healing is the love of God: God's love for you, and then your responsibility to extend His love to others**. We will study this for the next two days. Now, I want you to go to the Lord with all that has been written today regarding acceptance and ask the Lord to show you if you are failing in any of these areas. Then, in the space which follows, write down what God shows you and what you need to do about it.

O Beloved, unbelief, which is the root of all sin, is cured by belief, and belief brings healing.

DAY FIVE

God loves you with an everlasting, unconditional love. When you accept that truth and cling to it no matter what you endure, you will find yourself being healed. How well this is illustrated in the life of our own dear Dorie Van Stone. When I first met Dorie, she and I shared the platform at a conference given at Moody Bible Institute. Dorie was one of two daughters, the less attractive one. "The ugly one," Dorie says. Rejected by her mother while her sister was welcomed with open arms, Dorie was placed in an orphanage by her mother where she was beaten every single night. All sorts of abuse, including sexual abuse, went on in that orphanage, but it was there that Dorie first heard from a visiting church group that God loved her. Although she never felt love from anyone, in childlike faith, Dorie accepted the fact that God loved her. It was that one truth and her own little New Testament, given to her at that time, which held Dorie through years of much physical and emotional abuse. From the orphanage, Dorie was put in a foster home where she was nothing but a despised slave. It was believing God loved her that held her through the total rejection of her mother. Brought before a court to claim her child, Dorie's mom refused custody of Dorie, telling Dorie she wished she had never been born. It was believing the truth of God's love which held Dorie through the joy of finding her father, experiencing his love, and then being rejected by him because of her refusal to deny Jesus Christ. It was believing God's love and sovereignty that held Dorie through the sudden and unexpected death of her husband, Lloyd, at the age of sixty-two.

Read Dorie's book, *Dorie, The Girl Nobody Loved,* listen to her testimony on tape, and you will hear a living demonstration of the healing and enabling power of God's love when His love is believed and accepted.

Today, there are so many voices in the world, and even in Christendom, telling us that the root source of our problems is a lack of self-love and self-esteem. It sounds good, especially when it comes from the so-called experts, those who are trained in psychology and psychiatry, those who have earned degrees. It may even sound more plausible when it comes from those who have their degrees in psychiatry and/or psychology and are active Christians. It also seems to be truth if, or when, we see it in print—discussed, explained, and substantiated by other "experts" in magazines and books. But because it is in print and because many embrace it, does that make it true or right? If you think about it, you must say, "Of course not!" To know the truth regarding man, you and I must run to the plumb line of God's truth. Who knows man? Who made man? Who knows what makes man tick, what man needs? The answer to all of these questions is God! And since it is, then we need to go to God's Book and see what God has to say.

Nowhere, Beloved, does the Word of God tell us that our problem is lack of self-esteem, or lack of self-love, or a poor self-image. Instead, the Bible tells us that from the very beginning of the Garden of Eden, man's problem was unbelief. Unbelief, as you have already seen, caused man to sin. Sin separated man from God, and God is love. When man cuts himself off from love, he then begins the search to find a substitute. In this search, many hurts are incurred, many wounds inflicted. Self-love is that poor, but very deluding, substitute of God's love that deceptively puts man at the center instead of God. It is then that God exists for man, rather than man for God!

Self-love and self-esteem will teach you that you have worth and value apart from God. That, Beloved, is pride! It is the devil's lie! Self-love and self-esteem, some will tell you, must happen before you can love God or man. Or they will tell you that you can never love your neighbor until you love yourself.

These are subtle psychological distortions of the Word of God; distortions which you can fall into almost unknowingly if you do not stop and examine them carefully. This happened to me, because I found myself reading the works, listening to the tapes, and picking up the jargon of some who love God and who are being acclaimed as experts because people flock to listen to them and are helped to one degree or another. Although some are seemingly healed, it does not make the method or theory right or pleasing in the eyes of God. People are healed through psychic surgery, but that doesn't make it right. However, in the teaching of self-love and self-esteem, the reason you can be so subtly deceived is because these words and teachings are just a shade away from truth, but a shade that, if not discerned, will lead you further from the warmth of the Son into greater chilling darkness.

Acceptance of love is crucial to your healing, but it is acceptance of God's love rather than self-love. When you don't like who you are or what you have done, when the enemy comes whispering in your ear, knocking at the door of your mind, telling you that you are nothing, agree with your adversary, and then give him the truth. Tell him that apart from Jesus Christ you are nothing and you can do nothing that has any eternal worth or value. But also tell Satan that God loves you when you are nothing, accepts you just the way you are, and loves you with an everlasting, unconditional love that is in the process of transforming you into His image. Tell the devil that you are secure in God's love "because the love of God has been poured out within" your "heart through the Holy Spirit who was given to us" (Romans 5:5), and nothing "shall be able to separate" you "from the love of God, which is in Christ Jesus our Lord" (Romans 8:39).

Martin Luther had it right when he said, "God does not love us because we are valuable, but we are valuable because God loves us." "In this is love, not that we loved God, but that He loved us and sent His Son to be the propitiation for our sins. Beloved, if God so loved us, we also ought to love one another...if we love one another, God abides in us, and His love is perfected in us" (I John 4:10-12).

DAY SIX

The second truth you need to know in regard to acceptance of God's love as it affects your healing and the healing of others is that of your responsibility to allow God to love others through you.

Having believed and received the love of God and, thus, having His love poured out within our hearts, as Romans 5:5 says, we then become channels for His love, and the healing goes on and on! As I say this about His love going on and on, in my heart I can hear my friend, Sandi Patti, singing, "And the gift goes on." The song tells of the Father loving the Son, the Son loving us, and us then able to love. "We love because He first loved us" (I John 4:19).

How different this is from what so many are saying when they make the statement that self-love is the prerequisite and the criterion for our conduct towards our neighbor and that we cannot love God unless we first love ourselves. They say that our ability to love God, to love our neighbor, is limited by our ability to love ourselves; they say that we cannot love God more than we love our neighbor, and we cannot love our neighbor more than we love ourselves. So they are saying to love self, then neighbor, then God!

The way to love others is not to love self, but rather to love others, we must live in the light of death to self. Death to self causes me to take up my cross, deny myself, and follow Him.

1. Look up Mark 8:35-36. What is Jesus saying about our life in these verses?

2. What does Paul say regarding self in Galatians 2:20?

a. Write out Galatians 2:20, and begin memorizing it.

b. Now that you have written it out, in a sentence or two, explain how this verse fits in with what I have said to you today or how it agrees or disagrees with what the "self-love/self-esteem/self-image" proponents are saying. As I told you what they said, I was giving you almost direct quotes. I simply did not want to give you their names because that does not serve my purpose in this book on healing. I want to get you into the Bible, so that you can evaluate all you read and hear, including what I teach. No human teacher is infallible!

As you and I learn to live the crucified life, it will continually be death to self rather than love of self. As I say all of this, you may be asking, "But what about the command to love my neighbor as myself? Doesn't this mean I am to love myself?" I don't think so. Let's do a little investigation in the Word, so that you can see for yourself.

1. Look up Romans 13:8-10, and either write out the verses, or write the essence of what these verses are teaching.

2. Now read Mark 12:28-33.

3. In either of these passages which you have just looked up, is God telling you or commanding you to love yourself? What is He teaching about self in these verses?

4. Look up Philippians 2:3-8. Does this teach love of self or death to self? What, in essence, are these verses saying that would help us have a proper biblical opinion respecting self? As you answer this, do not miss Christ's example.

5. Now look up II Timothy 3:1-5. What do you learn in respect to love of self in this passage?

Some who try to support the view of self-love and self-esteem point to the Cross as a testimony of our worth and value, saying that if we did not have worth God would not have died for us. O Beloved, the Cross does not demonstrate our worth to God; it demonstrates God's unconditional love toward us. The Bible says, "God so loved the world, that He gave His only begotten Son...." It **does not say** that God so esteemed or saw the value of man that He gave His only begotten Son. A careful study of the Book of Romans, especially Chapter 9, will show us that in no way is God ever obligated to man. Rather our salvation is because of the pure mercy of God. "So then He has mercy on whom He desires, and He hardens whom He desires" (9:18). Salvation is purely and totally grace, and it, therefore, cannot be based on worth!

Please, please, when you present the gospel, do not present it on the basis of man's worth, for you would distort it. It is pure grace that pours out love "that saved a wretch like me," as John Newton, the writer of "Amazing Grace," so well worded it. "It is a trustworthy statement, deserving full acceptance, that Christ Jesus came into the world to save sinners, among whom I am foremost of all. And yet for this reason I found mercy..." (I Timothy 1:15,16). Sinners deserve hell. God in love, mercy and grace offers them heaven, a place and life where He will eternally express His love for us and where, at last, we will fitly be able to express ours for Him...because He first loved us!

O Beloved, will you not only accept His love, but will you accept your calling—the Cross—where you died to self, henceforth to live for God? And if you live for God, you will become a channel for His love to others. You will, as a branch, bear the fruit of love, not for self, but for others. And His love flowing through you will heal others.

There is a woman who wrote me sharing from a past that brought wound after wound. She wrote out her story for me, penning this note at the top of the yellow legal pad that she used, "Use whatever you want, whenever you need to. May God be glorified through all of this!" Let me share a little of her story, for it so well illustrates what we have been covering this week. Many of you will be able to relate to it in one way or another and learn from it. All of us will find it helpful in learning to love others to Christ and to healing.

"I never knew what maternal or paternal love was truly like. My parents were raised in homes where love was not expressed, and, consequently, we—my two brothers and one sister—were also raised this way. Of the four children, I seemed to be the one that was selected to be picked on. I was also the caretaker—I held everyone else together. I seemed to sense the rejection and lack of love, because at a very early age I began to try to destroy myself. This pattern lasted until I came to the Lord at thirty years of age."

Fired at with a shotgun by a drunken father, she was the maid, the cook, the housekeeper for her alcoholic parents and her siblings. She was the rescuer of her mother when her father would abusively rape her in a drunken rage. Sexually molested by her grandfather from the age of ten, she wrote, "I grew to hate sex because of the perverted way I saw it used. Now I saw it used in another way and grew to hate it even more. When my grandfather would take advantage of me, I was like a corpse. I was so full of fear. I became fearful of all men and became even more isolated. He had progressed from touching to intercourse, and I had digressed from being an innocent child to being an adult in a child's body. I felt abused in every way. To me, this was a fate worse than death. I was being tormented by the very people who were supposed to love and nurture me into adulthood. I felt like no one cared. I became a very angry child and began to act out my behavior in delinquent ways. I was so desperately looking for someone to care, but it seemed that no one did. God did—but at this point I had no idea Who He really was. I had only heard His name in cursing, not as my Father or as Someone Who cared about what happened to me. I got into serious trouble with the law for breaking into a house and stealing things."

Eventually in the sovereignty of God, through a bus ministry, this woman was exposed to God's people. What a lesson there is for us in tirelessly expressing God's unconditional love to others as she shares, "God brought many people into my life to draw me to Himself. I searched and searched but would never trust enough to totally let go and allow God to run my life. As soon as my parents noticed how much I enjoyed church, that was taken away."

At the age of seventeen, after a severe beating by her dad, she was placed in a foster home. "God knew what He was doing. They were neat Christian people." But "I ran away from anyone that required a commitment. Life became unbearable again." She attempted suicide, but it was to get attention. A year of Bible school followed with a godly couple taking a vested interest in her. After graduating from college with a degree in psychology, "I was still searching for the answer. I tried so hard to figure out why I was having problems.

"With all the psychology and head knowledge from the Bible, I still had no peace. In the meantime, I got involved in Precept and started studying with a fervor. I wanted so much to know Who God was and what purpose my life was to have. I began teaching emotionally disturbed children in school and drowned out my problems by helping them. I became even more depressed and suicidal. I shut all of my friends out. They would call me on the phone, but I would let it ring for hours. They would come over, and I would not go to the door. I began to reject anyone that tried to help. The old pattern had taken over again. I STILL HAD NOT DIED TO MYSELF. I wanted to run my life and let God have a little of it. A friend came over one evening and met me at the door as I was leaving.

"She backed me into the living room and sat down and tried to explain to me what I was doing to her and my other friends. It had never occurred to me that I was hurting anyone but myself. They really cared about me, but I did not believe them. My friend started crying, and I could not believe it. I had never had anyone cry over anything that I had done to myself. It blew me away.

"After she left I really began to examine my heart. I knew it was stone cold. God so convicted me and showed me my sin and just how selfish I really was. I decided then and there that it was time to let go and allow Him to totally control my life. I felt such a peace. The depression lifted, but the old patterns were hard to break. Through losing my job, I saw that my devotion is to be to Him totally. When I put other things before Him, He will weed them out and show me where my true devotion is to be.

"God has so changed my life. I no longer have to live under depression or with suicidal thoughts. THE CHOICE IS MINE. I am dead and no longer have to live that way. It has become a joy to live in freedom because I know that in and through Christ I can do anything that God requires of me.

"I still have to deal with the rejection, but I know God is there. He is, and was, in control and will not allow anything into my life that is not for my good, that is not for His glory, or that I cannot handle with His help. He is God! Who am I to question what He is doing? 'Therefore in Christ Jesus I have found reason for boasting in things pertaining to God. For I will not presume to speak of anything except what Christ has accomplished through me' (Romans 15:17-18)."

Beloved, there is a vital lesson in this testimony which you must not miss, and that is the constant need to cast all your care upon God. While I have not named every hurt with which you may have to deal, basically the cure will be found, in principle, in what we have covered and in what will be covered tomorrow. Every time a hurt arises, a pain occurs, a memory is triggered, you must humble yourself before God. Do not try to deal with it in your own strength or in your way. Jesus is there. You are yoked to Him. Roll that burden, that care, that anxiety, over onto His shoulders. He cares for you (I Peter 5:6-7).

DAY SEVEN

So many of our hurts center around a lack of acceptance. As I say this, I am sure that you can agree with me, for you remember the hurt which you have felt when others have not accepted you for what you were, or the hurt which came when others, in one way or another, rejected you. This is a hurt which comes **because we are not accepted by others**; and, therefore, to some degree or another we feel rejected. However, we can also experience hurt **because we do not accept others**. It is the second aspect of hurt, not accepting others, that we will deal with in our final day of study. As you remember, we dealt with rejection in week nine. These are the two aspects of acceptance that I want us to talk about today as we bring our study to a close.

This is the last area of hurt with which we will be dealing; however, it is very important. So don't slack in diligence, Beloved. You are almost over the finish line!

Many of our hurts have come, and unfortunately sometimes have continued, because we have failed to accept others as they are. People hurt because their parents, their husband or wife, their children, their friends, someone in their life, did not live up to or meet their expectations, desires, or ideals.

Let me summarize it this way. Generally we hurt and find it difficult to accept someone:

1. Because we feel (rightly or wrongly) that they owe us something, a "debt" they have not fulfilled—maybe love, respect, honor, time.

2. Because they are not what we wanted or expected in our relationship to them, e.g., as a father, mother, daughter, son, husband, wife, friend.

3. Because in their actions, their mannerisms, or their treatment of us, they remind us of someone who has hurt us, embittered us, failed us, or rejected us.

In other words, our hurt has come because we were the ones unable to accept others for one of the reasons I just mentioned. For instance, maybe you hurt because you never had the "Leave It To Beaver" or the "Father Knows Best" type of family life that you saw portrayed weekly on television while you were growing up.

Or you look at the Cosby Show and just wither inside because your Dad was never around, and when he was, he didn't want to be bothered with you. Maybe you even went to him and begged him for more attention. Maybe you told him there was a deep void in your life because he didn't hold you, touch you, wrestle with you, go to your games or school activities, or simply be and do what a father is to be and do. Maybe you got up the courage to express all of this, and he still didn't change. When that happens, the hurt seems even worse, for it is not as if he doesn't know your needs! Now he knows and still doesn't care to do that which is necessary to meet your needs! That seems like an even worse rejection—and, in a sense, it is.

Then "if" psychologists or psychiatrists come along and tell you that BECAUSE you have been deprived of your father's love and attention, you are going to have problems for the rest of your life, your hurt is only compounded. How depressing! How defeating! And it will be, Beloved, continually, hauntingly defeating and depressing until you accept your father just the way he is. The hurt and pain will continue not because he hasn't accepted you, but because you have not accepted him just the way he is. Your father's rejection of you, his unwillingness to meet your needs as his child, his lack of selfless love, is wrong, and he will stand accountable to the Heavenly Father. However, you cannot change him. What you can change, and no one else can do it for you, is your response to your father.

Healing won't come until you bow before God in meekness and accept the fact that this relationship has been permitted by God and has an eternal purpose. If it would have permanently damaged you, as the psychologist or psychiatrist might say, then God would have divinely intervened. Remember, my friend, and never forget that God's Word promises you that all things will work together for your good to conform you to His image.

I have used the illustration of a parent and child; however, as I am sure you realize, we could use other combinations of people, such as husband and wife, you and...whoever.

Now then, Beloved, I want you to take a few minutes to think about those people who trouble you in some way—from irritating you to being those you possibly want to shun or do not want to have anything to do with at all.

Make a list of their names. Then, considering the following five questions, write out the answers to those which are pertinent in respect to that person. You may have to use more paper than is provided. If so, do it, Beloved. I believe this exercise will be extremely beneficial.

1. What do you think _____ owes you?

2. What do you deserve in your relationship with _____ that you are not receiving or have never received?

3. Is the mold that you expect them to fit into one that you are sure God expects them to fit into?

4. Do you resent them because they remind you of someone? Who? How?

5. Do you project on others what is not there? Why?

Having done this, look up Romans 15:7, and write it out.

1. In what state were you, my friend, when Jesus Christ accepted you?

2. If you were to extend to these people the love of God which is within you, how would you respond to each of them? List their names, and then next to each, write out what you need to do to or with each one in order to be obedient to Romans 15:7.

3. Are you willing to forgive them? Remember love and forgiveness go together as do two ears, two nostrils, two eyes!

4. Now go back through your list of names and, one by one, tell God you will, in an act of faithful obedience, accept them as He and His Son have accepted them.

Well, Beloved, I cannot believe our thirteen weeks together are already complete. I want to thank you for hanging in there and for diligently studying God's Word. Your tenacity in completing and studying all of these aspects of your relationship to God and to man and your responsibility to properly deal with your emotions and your thoughts is essential and foundational to your healing.

However, as I say all of this, my friend, the knowing of all these truths and principles will not bring about your healing. They must be applied moment by moment, opportunity by opportunity. If you cannot do that alone, do not be ashamed. God did not leave you alone; He made you a part of His Body. Ask your Father God to direct you to someone who knows the Word, who loves the Lord, and who will come alongside you to walk you through the truths of God's Word which need application in your life.

And above all, Beloved, do not let this be the end of your Bible study. I have been praying that you will get into a systematic study of God's Word. There are many good Bible studies available to Christians today. I would suggest you choose one which will teach you to dig into God's Word on your own so that you learn skills which will enable you to study and discern truth by yourself. I believe difficult days are in the future, and God's people need to know how to feed themselves. Of course, I would count it a privilege to continue to be your teacher in an indirect way through our Precept Upon Precept Bible Studies, our In and Out Bible Studies, and through our daily devotional study guide, *Your Day & Mine,* which is excellent for your daily quiet time.

An ongoing study in the Word is crucial as preventative medicine for the hurts of life which are bound to come. If the Word of God is the balm of Gilead, we cannot go without it! And it is!

May "grace and peace be multiplied to you in the knowledge of God and of Jesus our Lord; seeing that His divine power has granted to us everything pertaining to life and godliness, through the true knowledge of Him who called us by His own glory and excellence. For by these He has granted to us His precious and magnificent promises, in order that by them you might become partakers of the divine nature, having escaped the corruption that is in the world by lust" (II Peter 1:2-4).

"For behold, the day is coming, burning like a furnace;
and all the arrogant and every evildoer will be chaff;
and the day that is coming will set them ablaze," says
the LORD of hosts, "so that it will leave them neither
root nor branch. But for you who fear My name the
sun of righteousness will rise with healing in its
wings; and you will go forth and skip about like calves
from the stall. And you will tread down the wicked,
for they shall be ashes under the soles of your feet
on the day which I am preparing," says the LORD of
hosts (Malachi 4:1-3).

My heart is filled with His love for you.

ATTRIBUTES OF GOD

Omniscient — God knows all. He has a perfect knowledge of everything that is past, present, or future. Job 37:16 and Psalm 139:1-6.

Omnipotent — God possesses all power. He is able to bring into being anything that He has decided to do, with or without the use of any means. Genesis 18:14; Job 42:2; Jeremiah 32:27.

Omnipresent — God is present everywhere, in all the universe, at all times, in the totality of His character. Proverbs 15:3 and Jeremiah 23:23,24.

Eternal — God has no beginning, and He has no end. He is not confined to the finiteness of time or of man's reckoning of time. He is, in fact, the cause of time. Deuteronomy 32:40 and Isaiah 57:15.

Immutable — God is always the same in His nature, His character, and His will. He never changes, and He can never be made to change. Psalm 102:25-27; Malachi 3:6; and Hebrews 13:8.

Incomprehensible — Because God is God, He is beyond the understanding of man. His ways, character, and acts are higher than ours. We only understand as He chooses to reveal. Job 11:7; Isaiah 55:8-9; Romans 11:33.

Self-Existent — There is nothing upon which God depends for His existence except Himself. The whole basis of His existence is within Himself. There was a time when there was nothing but God Himself. He added nothing to Himself by creation. Exodus 3:14 and John 5:26.

Self-Sufficient — Within Himself, God is able to act — to bring about His will without any assistance. Although He may choose to use assistance, it is His choice not His need. Psalm 50:7-12 and Acts 17:24,25.

Infinite — The realm of God has no limits or bounds whatsoever. I Kings 8:27 and Psalm 145:3.

Transcendent — God is above His creation, and He would exist if there were no creation. His existence is totally apart from His creatures or creation. Isaiah 43:10 and 55:8,9.

Sovereign — God is totally, supremely, and preeminently over all His creation. There is not a person or thing that is not under His control and foreknown plan! Daniel 4:35.

Holy — God is a morally excellent, perfect being. His is purity of being in every aspect. Leviticus 19:2; Job 34:10; Isaiah 47:4; Isaiah 57:15.

Righteous — God is always good. It is essential to His character. He always does the right thing. Ultimately, since He is God, whatever He does is right. He is the absolute. His actions are always consistent with His character, which is love. Deuteronomy 32:4 and Psalm 119:142.

Just — In all of His actions, God acts with fairness. Whether He deals with man, angels, or demons, He acts in total equity by rewarding righteousness and punishing sin. Since He knows all, every decree is absolutely just. Numbers 14:18; 23:19; Psalm 89:14.

Merciful — God is an actively compassionate being. In His actions, He responds in a compassionate way toward those who have opposed His will in their pursuit of their own way. Psalms 62:12; 89:14; 116:5; Romans 9:14-16.

Longsuffering — God's righteous anger is slow to be kindled against those who fail to listen to His warnings or to obey His instructions. The eternal longing for the highest good for His creatures holds back His holy justice. Numbers 14:18 and 2 Peter 3:9.

Wise — God's actions are based on His character which allows Him to choose righteous ends and to make fitting plans to achieve those ends. Isaiah 40:28 and Daniel 2:20.

Loving — The attribute of God which causes Him to give Himself for another, even to the laying down of His own life. This attribute causes Him to desire the other's highest good without any thought for Himself. This love is not based upon the worth, response, or merit of the object being loved. Jeremiah 31:3; Romans 5:8; I John 4:8.

Good — This attribute of God causes Him to give to others in a way which has no motive and is not limited by what the recipients deserve. 2 Chronicles 5:13 and Psalm 106:1.

Wrathful — There is within God a hatred for all that is unrighteous and an unquenchable desire to punish all unrighteousness. Whatever is inconsistent with Him must ultimately be consumed. Exodus 34:6,7; 2 Chronicles 19:2; Romans 1:18.

Truthful — All that God says is reality. Whether believed by man or not, whether seen as reality or not, if it is spoken by God, it is reality. Whatever He speaks becomes truth as we know it. Psalm 31:5 and Titus 1:2.

Faithful — God is always true to His promises. He can never draw back from His promises of blessing or of judgment. Since He cannot lie, He is totally steadfast to what He has spoken. Deuteronomy 7:9 and 2 Timothy 2:13.

Jealous — God is unwilling to share His glory with any other creature or give up His redeemed people. Exodus 20:5; 34:14.

Notes

Chapter 3

1. Douglas, J. D., *The New Bible Dictionary* (Grand Rapids, Michigan; Wm. B. Eerdmans Publishing Co., 1962), p. 469.
2. Vincent, Marvin R., *Word Studies in the New Testament, Volume IV* (Grand Rapids, Michigan: Wm. B. Eerdmans Publishing Company, 1969), p. 318.
3. Ibid., p. 318.

Chapter 10

4. Bobgan, Martin and Deidre, *How To Counsel From Scripture* (Chicago: Moody Press, 1985), p. 8.

Chapter 12

5. Richards, Lawrence O., *Expository Dictionary of Bible Words,* Regency Reference Library (Grand Rapids, Michigan: Zondervan, 1985), p. 46.
6. Ibid., p. 46.
7. Vine, W. E., *Expository Dictionary of New Testament Words,* 3rd edition (Nashville, Tennessee: Thomas Nelson Publishers, 1983), p. 47-48.

Chapter 13

8. Vine, W. E., *Expository Dictionary of New Testament Words,* 3rd edition (Nashville, Tennessee: Thomas Nelson Publishers, 1983), p. 727.